Reformed Social Ethics and the Korean Church

Asian Thought and Culture

Sandra Wawrytko
General Editor

Vol. 21

PETER LANG
New York • Washington, D.C./Baltimore • Boston
Bern • Frankfurt am Main • Berlin • Vienna • Paris

Nak Heong Yang

Reformed Social Ethics and the Korean Church

PETER LANG
New York • Washington, D.C./Baltimore • Boston
Bern • Frankfurt am Main • Berlin • Vienna • Paris

Library of Congress Cataloging-in-Publication Data

Yang, Nak Heong.
Reformed social ethics and the Korean church/ Nak Heong Yang.
p. cm. — (Asian thought and culture; vol. 21)
Includes bibliographical references and index.
1. Presbyterian Church—Korea—Doctrines—History. 2. Christian ethics—Korea—History. 3. Social ethics—Korea—History. 4. Sociology, Christian (Reformed Church)—Korea—History. 5. Reformed Church—Korea—Doctrines—History. 6. Church and state—Korea—History. 7. Christianity and politics—Presbyterian Church—History. 8. Korea—Church history.
I. Title. II. Series.
BX9151.K8Y36 261.7'09519—dc20 94-30285
ISBN 0-8204-2622-9
ISSN 0893-6870

Die Deutsche Bibliothek-CIP-Einheitsaufnahme

Yang, Nak Heong:
Reformed social ethics and the Korean church/ Nak Heong Yang.
– New York; Washington, D.C./Baltimore; Bern; Frankfurt am Main; Berlin; Vienna; Paris: Lang.
(Asian thought and culture; Vol. 21)
ISBN 0-8204-2622-9
NE: GT

The paper in this book meets the guidelines for permanence and durability of the Committee on Production Guidelines for Book Longevity of the Council of Library Resources.

Printed in the United States of America.

To my family,
Youngae, Geepeom and Yeeun

CONTENTS

Acknowledgements

This book was originally written as a doctoral dissertation at Fuller Theological Seminary. My study in the United States would have been impossible without the support of the Seoul Youngdong Presbyterian Church. For more than four years, the congregation of that church faithfully provided me with finances and prayer. Among members, I give special thanks to Dr. Bong Ho Son who played a decisive roles for my further study in the United States.

It seems a special providence of God that I was mentored by Dr. Mouw. For an international student who should confront a different language and culture, he showed an ideal model of mentorship through an unchanging attitude of understanding, kindness, and encouragement. In spite of a moutain of duties as a Provost and president elect, he was always ready to meet my need for guidance. He was my mentor in Christian Ethics not merely through theory but through practice.

I am grateful to Dr. Mahn Yol Yi for his supervising me in chapter Four which discussed the Korean church-state relationship. I also thank my American friends, Noel Taylor, Phil Corr, Tom Phitzenmayer, Robert Cornwall, and Norman Gordon for reading one or two chapters of my dissertation for proof-reading. They will remain in my memory as good Christian models who willingly gave help to an international student in the midst of their own doctoral study or job.

My friend Jong Soo Han's kindness is unforgettable. He helped me at the last moment of printing out the dissertation by providing me with all the necessary equipments.

I am aware that throughout all the stages of doctoral study, there were innumerable prayers of my friends and relatives. Although I cannot enumerate all of their names here, I send my heartfelt thanks to them, especially to my mother and father who spent many nights praying for me.

Lastly, but foremostly, I express the greatest gratitude to my wife Young Ae. During those years of my study in a foreign land, she was the only person who was always with me and beside me. Throughout all the difficulties and discouragements, she was the one who encouraged and prayed for me. Only God knows how crucial have been her companionship and her prayers for me. All glory be to God who worked behind all these human agents and incidents according to his good will.

Prologue

Except at the very first stage of Protestant evangelism in Korea, the political theories and practices of the majority of Korean presbyterian churches have failed to represent the Reformed tradition. Under the name of "separation of church and state" or in the pretext of concentrating on the "primary" duty of the church, the evangelism, they have not taken their prophetic responsibilities to warn the state of its injustice. Despite their claim for "political neutralism," they publicly expressed their approval for the unjust government which attemted to destroy the democracy of the nation.

The political outlook of Calvin and his followers was drastically different from that of the evangelical Korean presbyterian churches. Consistently taking a very positive stance toward politics and government, Calvin reproached the Anabaptists as "fanatics" because they condemned them.

Although Calvin stressed the Christian responsibility of obeying the political authorities, it was never an unqualified obedience. Christians had to disobey the ruler's commands which contradicted the divine commands. Even though Calvin was far less radical than his successors, such as Knox and Beza who fully endorsed the Chriatian right and duty of active resistance to unjust authorities, he emphasized the church's duty as a watchman over the state. With his fellow Genevan pastors, Calvin rigorously exercised his prophetic responsibility by sharply criticizing the injustice of the rulers.

Differently from Koreans' common understanding of the phrase "separation of chuch and state," the original intent of the First Amendment was not to deter the church from expressing her prophetic opinions on the critical social-political issues in which matters of important morality was at stake, but to ban the (partial) support by the state of the church(es).

INTRODUCTION

According to the statistics of 1992, the number of Korean Christians runs to the tens of million. Among them, Presbyterians are in the absolute majority: they comprise about two thirds of all Korean Christians.[1] Of these, with only one significant exception, almost all Korean Presbyterian denominations can be classified as theologically 'conservative.' They claim to be heirs of the orthodox Calvinistic theology and tradition. In fact, such words as 'Reformed,' 'Calvinistic,' orthodox and conservative are the most popular adjectives for the names of the scores of Korean Presbyterian denominations.

It is true that, in some theological aspects, conservative Korean Presbyterians follow the Reformed tradition. For instance, they emphasize the Reformed distinctives of *sola gratia, sola fide,* and *sola scriptura.* They accept the sovereignty of God in salvation history as well as the doctrines of predestination and election. They recognize that men and women are justified only by grace through faith in Jesus Christ. In addition, they elevate the authority of the Bible and stress the centrality of the preaching in worship.

With these Reformed elements in the Korean Presbyterian churches, they still seem to be lacking one of the essential aspects of the Reformed tradition; that is, they lack a consistent concern for the larger community in which they live. As a result, there is the absence of a Christian social ethic. To many Korean conservative Presbyterians, it sounds strange that the Reformed tradition has a concern for society. For them, the Christian religion relates only to individual, spiritual, and ecclesiastical affairs. In their understanding, Reformed theology is little more than a discussion of soteriology, that is, the doctrine of the salvation of individual souls. Is this a proper understanding of the Reformed tradition and theology? This is the principal question I wish to explore throughout this dissertation.

As most Korean Presbyterians know, one of the characteristics of the Reformed theology has been its emphasis on God's sovereignty. This sovereignty applies to all that God has created. He is the Lord of the world as well as of the church. As the ruler of everything he intends every sphere of human life to be ordered according to his will. Reformed Christians, believing that God has a design for society, are deeply concerned about leading their communal life according to Gods will.

Thus, Calvin not only aimed at saving souls in Geneva, but he sought a "Geneva that was reformed by the Word of God."As one historian of Calvinism observes:

> In Scotland and in England the Reformed community sought to build the New Jerusalem. The Puritans who came to New England were not simply seeking freedom to worship God as they liked. They wer going on an errand into the wilderness to establish a Christian society an to demonstrate to the decadent society of Europe the possibilities of a Christian community. [2]

In many cases, concern for one's community leads to concern for politics. This is because politics is what affects most the life of a society. In the underdeveloped and developing countries particularly, everything, including economics, is decisively influenced by the political situation of the country. Accordingly, those people who are concerned about the conditions and destiny of their people cannot avoid being interested in the political situation of their country.

Many Korean Presbyterians argue, however, that those who are interested in holiness had better not be interested in politics.[3] Although few Koreans have overtly expressed this view, there lies in the subconsciousness of most Koreans the conviction that only those who are ambitious to gain power become interested in politics. This negative reaction to politics is understandable when we take into account the fact that, historically, political power has been abused in Korea almost without exception. Koreans have had little experience with rulers who use their power for the good of the people. Christians in Korea are unconsciously influenced by this negative experience of politics and political power. Because of this historical background, Korean Christians have come to believe that Christians who are interested in politics and aspire to political power are uncouth and are endangering their souls.

The sequence of logic for most Korean Presbyterians would be something like this: if one becomes concerned about society, he or she will unavoidably get interested in politics. Once involved in politics, he or she would want to have political power to accomplish his/her goal. In pursuing political power, he or she would most likely be corrupted. As a result, the salvation of his/her soul would be jeopardized.[4]

Here arises a question on the nature of politics: is political power always an object of sinful craving? Is it inescapable that whoever gets involved in politics become corrupted and that whoever becomes politically influential abuses his/her position? Does the Bible teach that it is impossible for politics to be used properly, that is, for the common good and glory of God? Historically, have the Calvinists taught that the political order and political institutions are intrinsically evil?

In the first half of my dissertation, I will show that Calvinism has always answered these questions with a "no." In the second half, I will examine the way Korean Presbyterian churches have taught and acted in politically critical situations. I will show that with the exception a few attempts by a small number of early Korean Presbyterians, the Korean Presbyterian churches have failed to properly fulfill their socio-political responsibilities.

It would not be fair, however, to maintain that all conservative Korean Presbyterian leaders teach that Christians should never be involved in politics. Rather, some of them assert that on the individual level Christians should participate in politics to realize the sovereignty of God in all realms of life. If Christians avoid participating in politics because it is considered "dirty," declares Myung Hyuk Kim, a leading professor at a conservative Presbyterian seminary in Korea, it would be equivalent to giving politics over to Satan. "Politics too is our realm under God's sovereignt."[5] Chong Yoon Lee, a leading Presbyterian pastor, also affirms that Christians may "actively" participate in politics "on the individual level."[6] At least to this extent, Korean Presbyterians can be said to be faithful to the Reformed tradition.

When it comes to the Christian political witness on the corporate level, however, most Korean Presbyterian leaders raise objections. "It should not be allowed for the church to be involved in politics", states Chong Yoon Lee, "because it is the violation of the principle of the sphere sovereignty, and the principle of separation of church and state."[7] "The pastors should keep silent on the political issues," states Han Hum Og, another well-known Korean Presbyterian pastor, "because they are the public persons who represent their churches." If they want to speak on politics, he continues, "let them do so after resigning their positions at church."[8]

Those who object to the political witness of the church as an institution base their argument on the principle of "separation of church and state." It is true that this principle appears in the Korean Constitution, which in turn, was probably adopted from the United States. As will be shown in chapter six, the First Amendment to the U. S. Constitution originally sought to ban government aid to religion, including the establishment of a state church.[9] Lacking this historical information, conservative Korean Presbyterians have uncritically taken the phrase verbatim (as do many American Christians), as if it were a sacred phrase in the Bible. Grounded in their misconception of the intention of that phrase, they have insisted that the church should never "meddle in" or "interfere with" politics.

It is not always very clear, however, what Korean Presbyterians mean when they refer to churchly " interference" or "meddling" in politics. In other words, how much, or to what extent, is the principle of separation of church and state to be applied in real life? Do they mean by that concept, as Bong Ho Son maintains, that pastors should not participate in the "party politics" in such a way as to express their support for a particular candidate running for a public office?[10] If this is the case, there would be no serious problem. They do not stop there, however, but go on to insist that the church, as a church, should never express their socio-political concerns publicly in words or deeds. Does this represent the authentic Reformed position on the issue of church and state? Have Calvinists historically taught that the church as well as pastors should not speak to the state on public issues? And indeed, have they espoused the position of political quietism?

The result of my study on the Reformed tradition shows that it is not so. The fact is, Reformed churches have seldom shied away from speaking to the state as a church on public issues. As Fred Graham makes clear, Calvin's church in Geneva so rigorously exercised its right to speak "as a church to the state" that the form of government in Geneva was sometimes called a "theocracy."[11] With "a vast, all-encompassing concern for the way the government handled its affairs," Calvin and the other pastors were "constantly stepping into the political circle both as individuals and as representatives of the church in Geneva."[12]

Although it is seldom officially verbalized, the insistence by Korean evangelical Presbyterians that the church, as a church, should not voice its position on socio-political issues appears to stem from the fear that such a statement would not only impair the holiness of the church but also divert the church from its so-called "primary" duty, namely, evangelism. Is this really true? Is the effort for evangelism really destined to contradict Christian social concern? Are the churches that seek to take a responsible stance on socio-political issues necessarily weakened in their evangelical zeal? I will show in chapter three why modern representative Reformed scholars believe that social concern helps our evangelistic efforts and in fact constitutes an important part of this effort.

The "contradiction," in fact, exists not between evangelical zeal and the church's socio-political concern, but rather between the Korean Presbyterian churches' theory and practice with regard to political issues. During the last several decades, Korean Presbyterian churches have maintained that the church should not be involved in politics and that, therefore, they should abstain from any expression of their views on political issues. Nevertheless, they did not hesitate, in some critical moments, to express their support and approval for the government. What made the matter more regrettable was that they issued such statements of endorsement on the occasions when the government made decisions that most thinking Koreans considered to be seriously unjust. I will describe several of these cases in detail in chapter five.

Even when Korean Presbyterians could not but admit that the government's actions were seriously unjust, they refused to play the prophetic role by criticizing or warning the government of its unrighteousness. Romans 13:1-7 has always been used as one of the main theological justifications for their political quietism. They have insisted that the apostle Paul, in this Scriptural passage, commanded Christians to render an absolute obedience to the ruling authorities, and that he himself practiced his instruction by never questioning the legitimacy of the tyrannical Roman emperors. Therefore, they argued, Christians should obey even the unjust government, and the church should not venture to say anything against the government. One of the main questions I raise in this dissertation relates to this very attitude by the Korean Presbyterian churches. Is this really the Reformed position? In other words, have the Reformers who formulated the Calvinist tradition taught that Christians should render an unqualified obedience to the government?

The best way to answer this question, of course, would be to directly investigate the political writings of some representative Calvinists such as John Calvin, Theodore Beza, Calvin's immediate successor in Geneva, and John Knox, the father of the Scottish Reformation. No one will question that these are three of the most authoritative figures in the history of Calvinism. My research of their writings on Christian obedience to the temporal authorities has demonstrated that the Reformed tradition does not espouse unquestioning obedience to political authorities. On the contrary, prototypical Calvinists invariably taught that there were some cases where Christians ought not obey the civil authorities. Moreover, at certain points, resistance to them was permitted. Theodore Beza's and John Knox's positions on this issue are particularly radical, while Calvin's is not as radical as his disciples. But even the relatively conservative Calvin would appear in the eyes of Korean Presbyterians as being very political and radical. Calvin admitted that there were several cases for Christian disobedience and resistance to unjust rulers. By so doing he opened the door for later Calvinists to be far more radical in their resistance to tyrants.

Thus, the first two chapters of my dissertation aim to discuss the ideas of Calvin, Knox and Beza on the nature of Christian obedience to secular authorities. Chapter one will analyze Calvin's last chapter on civil government in his *Institutes of the Christian Religion* as well as relevant sections of his commentaries. In the second chapter, I will be dealing with several of the political writings by Knox and Beza.

By examining these three preeminent leaders of the Reformed tradition, we can grasp how the early Reformed tradition on the issue of Christian obedience to secular power was established. It would not be sufficient, however, to investigate only the sixteenth-century Calvinist position. We also need to know whether modern Calvinists still maintain the earlier Calvinist position or have abandoned it. The third chapter intends, therefore, to show that modern Calvinists have faithfully held to and even further developed their forefathers' position in this regard. They do not stop at discussing the limit of Christian obedience to the secular power, but they proceed to work out a Christian strategy for social reform. In contrast to those conservative evangelicals who emphasize exclusively the importance of evangelism either for the salvation of souls or as a strategy for the social reform, modern Calvinists realize the necessity of Christian social involvement and political witness. My discussion of the modern Calvinist position on Christian socio-political responsibility will be limited, however, to the circle of modern Anglo-American scholars.

The purpose of this project is to assess and evaluate how closely the theory and practice of Korean Presbyterian churches have followed the Reformed tradition in terms of taking socio-political responsibilities.

Therefore, chapters four and five examine the socio-political theories and practices of Korean Christians, particularly Presbyterians, during the century after the coming of the Gospel to Korea in 1884. The focus will be laid on the Korean Presbyterian response to the critical moments of Korean history. In the final chapter, I will try to reveal the reasons why such a great gap has come into existence, particularly after 1945, between the theory and practice of the historical Reformed position and that of the Korean Presbyterian churches.

The discussion of this dissertation is limited to the analysis of the conservative Korean Presbyterian churches' theories and practices on the above-said issues. That is to say, I do not intend to examine the political positions of the more radical and 'liberal' Presbyterian proponents of the internationally-known "*minjung* theology."[13] To criticize and evaluate their theories would require another voluminous work. It should suffice here to say that, to me, they seem to be going to the opposite extreme by seeming to make "politics" everything: they tend to make the issues of this world their sole concern.

In the end, I do not conclude that politics is the only or most important Christian duty, rather I wish to prove that by expressing adequate concern for the community at large, Christians are able to fulfill the commandment of Jesus. He calls us to "love your neighbor as youself." Without doing this, I believe, the church loses much of its "taste" in this world.

1 See *Kidogkyo Daeyonkam* (Seoul: Kidogkyomoonsa, 1992), 277-296.

2 John H. Leith, *Introduction to the Reformed Tradition* (Atlanta, Georgia: John Knox Press, 1981), 76. See also Perry Miller, *Errand into the Wilderness* (Cambridge: The Balknap Press of Harvard University Press, 1956).

3 In an answer of Bong-Ho Son, a representative intellectual of conservative Korean presbyterian church, to a question raised by an audience in a conference on church and state issue. Myung Hyuk Kim et al., eds., *Modern Church and State* (Seoul: Emmao Publishing Co., 1988), 121.

4 Since it is difficult to find writings on the topic of Christians and politics written by conservative Korean Christians, I draw this from my own observation and experience of the attitude and values of Korean Christians.

5 Myung Hyuk Kim, A Historical Survey of the Relationship between Church and State, *Church and State* (Seoul, 1988), 112-113.

6 Chong Yoon Lee, Church and State from the Perspective of the Bible, *Modern Church and State* (Seoul, 1988), 84-85.

7 *Ibid.*

8 Han Hum Og, The Responsibility of the Church for the Political Participation of the Lay People, *Modern Church and State*, 33. Og seems to contradict himself on this point, for he argues in the same essay that pastors are responsible to provide lay persons with the biblical guidance and principles on political issues and that it was wrong for him to have kept silence on the death of Chong Chul Park, a Korean college student who was killed by the torture of police. *Ibid.*, 30.

9 The original intent of the separation of church and state in the First Amendment will be discussed in detail in chapter six.

10 Bong Ho Son's answer to a question by an audience. Myung Hyuk Kim et at., eds., *Modern Church and State*, 121.

11 W.Fred Graham, *The Constructive Revolutionary John Calvin: His Socio-Economic Impact* (Michigan State University Press, 1987), 176.

12 *Ibid.*, 160-159.

[13] The presbyterian denomination, which is called 'Kijang' has around 300,000 members. It is much less than five percent of all Korean presbyterians. *kidogkyo Daeyonkam*, 278.

CHAPTER I

CALVIN AND POLITICAL AUTHORITY

What was John Calvin's attitude toward the politics? Did he take a stance of indifference to it like so many Christians today, or did he teach that Christians, as individuals and as church, should take political responsibility? In particular, how did he think the Christian church should respond to unjust and tyrannical political authority? To what extent is his instruction on this subject applicable to contemporary political life? These are the main questions to which I will attempt to give answers in this chapter.

Calvin and Politics

Calvin was living in an age when a crisis was occurring in the Christian understanding of politics.[1] Early reformers' attack on the papacy resulted in the discrediting of some essential elements of political practice such as institution, power, and domination. In such a context, Calvin undertook a task of restoring the moral status of politics.

In formulating his political theory, Calvin's most obvious opponents were Anabaptists. The *Institutes* were written at the time of the sanguinary Muenster episode, and after years of Anabaptist propaganda which had asserted that the Christian is not properly a citizen in an earthly state and has nothing to do with civil government.[2] For Calvin this was a dangerous heresy.

Anabaptists were divided into two groups of radicals in their attitude toward politics. On the one hand, there were extremists who may well have been called "separatists" or "spiritualists." Thinking that the freedom of the gospel acknowledges neither king nor magistrate nor law among humans, "but looks to Christ alone," they insisted that no power should be set up over them.[3] Calvin describes their attitude toward politics in the *Institutes*:

> ...after we have died through Christ to the elements of this world (Col. 2:20), are transported to God's kingdom, and sit among heavenly beings, it is a thing unworthy of us and set far beneath our excellence to be occupied with those vile and worldly cares which have to do with business foreign to a Christian man.[4]

In short, they thought that it was not appropriate for holy and pious people to have concern for such an earthly and carnal thing as politics.

On the other hand, there was another group of radicals, the followers of Thomas Muentzer. These were another kind of extremists obsessed with an idea that the whole world should be "reshaped" to a new form, that is, in the image of a pure communion of saints. That goal could be achieved, they thought, by overthrowing the corrupted world and rooting out its vicious elements. For that purpose, they argued, a "holy violence" was justified.

Thus, whether peaceful or bloody, they had one thing in common, the anti-political impulse. With their ultimate purpose of preserving "the purity" of their church in a "polluted" world, they denied any obligations to the political order. They sought, rather, to escape from it.

Luther also drew a sharp contrast between the two forms of power, "spiritual" and "secular." He denied that there were any elements common to both. "Spiritual" power was practiced through the means of suasion over the consciences of the believers. It could not carry with it any civil penalties. Of political institutions and personalities, however, he was suspicious and even at times contemptuous. Wolin, while overstating the case, does rightly identify a tendency in Luther's thought to denigrate politics. For Luther, he declares,

> Secular government thus stood alone, but undignified, as the sole embodiment of an effective ordering discipline; it was the major cohesive force in society. Despite its practical importance, the political province was not that of a Christian virtue, but of coercion and repression.[5]

In a word, hostility towards the political order was also a part of Luther's outlook. The result of these condemnations of "worldly power" was that a whole tradition of order and civility was jeopardized.

In the midst of this trend of despising political order, what Calvin undertook was the task of rescuing the reputation of politics and softening the black-and-white contrasts between the civil order and the religious order. By reminding the Protestants of the political side of their nature and educating them in the rudiments of politics, he led them to understand that an element of power was needed to insure the coherence and solidarity of the society. For the preservation of "humanity," he thought, politics was an indispensable element.[6]

As John McNeill declares, few theologians have had such a high esteem of politics as Calvin, or, have shown so much attention to political affairs.[7] He believed that man and woman become more political when they are motivated by religion.[8] With his vast, all-encompassing concern for the way the government handled its affairs, he was "constantly stepping into the political circle" both as an individual and as a representative of the church in Geneva.[9]

Calvin did not believe that political and religious matters could be ultimately separated. Rather, he understood church and state to be coterminous. It was self-evident for him that the church should be concerned for the whole of life. Accordingly, he did not regard politics as a matter remote from religion. Of course, he agreed that "Christ's spiritual kingdom and the civil jurisdiction are things completely distinct,"[10] yet he considered it a mere fanaticism to consider "the whole nature of government" to be "a thing polluted, which has nothing to do with Christians."[11] Since Christians require the help of the political order during their pilgrimage upon the earth, declares Calvin, taking it from them is no less than depriving them of their "humanity" itself. He was so outraged by the Anabaptists' attempt to abolish the civil government that he criticized it as an "outrageous barbarity."[12]

Unlike Luther who understood the state to be a mighty engine for repression,[13] he refused to see it as a kind of necessary evil, or nothing more than a remedy for human perversity.[14] For him, government was not a mere concession to sin which must be tolerated. On the contrary, it was an "excellent and beneficial institution" from God.[15] He argues that the function of government among human beings is "no less than that of bread, water, sun, and air." Its place of honor is "far more excellent" than those.[16] The reason is obvious: it keeps "humanity" from being degenerated into brutality. Calvin warns repeatedly that rejection of the government would lead the human society into an "animal-like anarchy." God's purpose in instituting government was, for Calvin, to prevent humans from living "like dogs and cats."[17]

Obedience to the Political Authority

One of the main emphases of Calvin with regard to the civil government is the divine origin of political authority. Faithfully following the Pauline passage in Romans 13:1-7, he believes that all powers are from God. This is his starting point in the discussion of Christian obedience and resistance to the political authorities. The magistrates are in their positions not "by their own strength" but "by divine providence and holy ordinance." They "have been placed there by the hand of the Lord."[18] As "ministers" and "representatives of God" they have been "invested with divine authority." Calvin exalts the office of the magistracy so much as to give an impression that he regards it as retaining more sanctity than that of the pastors: "...civil authority is a calling, not only holy and lawful before God, but also the most sacred and by far the most honorable of all callings in the whole life of mortal men."[19]

The implication of the high dignity of the magistrates is for Calvin that the subjects should honor them as "God's vicegerents." "The first duty of subjects toward their magistrates is," says Calvin, "to think most honorably of their office," and "to esteem and reverence them." The word "honor" includes, of course, subjection to the civil authorities.[20]

Resistance to the magistrates is resistance to God. It is the natural corollary of Calvin's premise that the ruler's power is from God. To resist authority is none other than to "despise the providence of God," and, indeed, an attempt to "overturn the order of God." Such evil acts never "go unpunished" but "cause the ruin" by incurring "God's condemnation" and "every act of God's vengeance."[21]

Taking such a strong stand on the duty of subjects to obey the political authority, Calvin did not allow any possibility of resistance to the ruler on the private citizen's level. Furthermore, he insisted that subjects should even obey the tyrants without complaint. Here he makes the case in an unqualified manner:

> We are not only subject to the authority of princes who perform their office toward us uprightly and faithfully but also to the authority of all who, by whatever means, have got control of affairs, even though they perform not a bit of the prince's office.... whoever they may be, they have their authority solely from him.[22]

> Though we were under Turks, under tyrants, and under the deadly enemies of the Gospel, yet it is commanded us to submit ourselves unto them. Why so? Even because it pleaseth God.[23]

To Calvin, the question of legitimacy of power is not so important. To ask by what right those who are in authority came by their power is an "empty curiosity." "It ought really to be sufficient for us that they rule." No matter "by whatever means" they have gained control of affairs, if only it is evident that the kingdom has been given to them, we ought to "serve" them.[24] In other words, for Calvin, "the authority of the prince is the authority of *de facto*."[25] The fact that someone is the incumbent ruler stands for the full legitimacy of power. Or as F. J. C. Hearshaw puts it, the political authority is to be obeyed "not because it is legitimate according to some text which can be applied by human reason, but simply because it exists. Its legitimacy is implied in its existence, because it could not exist without the will of God."[26] In this respect Calvin shows himself to be a thorough realist.

Not only the matter of legitimacy but the character of the rulers also is not to affect the duty of subjects to obey them. Subjects should revere "all their rulers...in the highest degree, whatever they may be like." As the "noble and divine power" resides even in "a most wicked tyrant," a king who is "utterly unworthy of all honor," and in "the most unworthy men" who degrade the authority of magistrates "as much as they can with their own wickedness," subjects should be willing to acknowledge them as powers ordained by God.[27] A typical example in Scripture of such a tyrant is, for Calvin, "that abominable and cruel tyrant" Nebuchadnezzar, the Babylonian king who conquered Judah and Jerusalem in the sixth century B.C. According to Jeremiah 27: 5-8, Calvin maintains, God commanded the Jews to pay obedience even to such a tyrannical ruler "for no other reason than that he possessed the kingship."[28]

It would be unfair to deny that Calvin has a conservative bias when he maintains that people "should learn not to examine the men themselves." It is "seditious thought," states Calvin, that a king should be treated "according to his merit."[29] At this point Calvin seems far more conservative than Aquinas who argued that the extreme tyrant should be deposed even by the use of violence.[30] As Hoepfl points out, in Calvin "... even the familiar medieval distinction between the tyrant by title and the tyrant by practice" is not allowed to stand.[31]

The Tyrant as a Curse for the Wicked People

If, as Calvin argues, even the tyrants are as equal before God as the righteous and faithful princes, why does God send such evil rulers? How does it happen that legitimate but tyrannical governors are sometimes sent to rule over us? Calvin's answer to this question is a harsh one:

> ...they who rule unjustly and incompetently have been raised up by him to punish the wickedness of the people....a wicked king is the Lord's wrath upon the earth.... For Scripture reckons all such calamities [as a robber who seizes your possessions, an adulterer who pollutes your marriage bed, or a murderer who seeks to kill you] among God's curses.[32]

Briefly, the wicked rulers are "whips of the Lord," instruments of judgment of God. They are sent to scourge the community for its sins; their coming ought to provoke a sense of collective guilt among the people. Therefore, when people "are cruelly tormented by a savage prince," they should "be mindful of their own misdeeds" searching their consciences for the sins they had committed.[33]

The result of this religious interpretation of the tyrant is, as Wolin shrewdly points out, that the relationship between the tyrant and the subjects transcends ordinary political categories, for the concept of sin is not a political conception at all. Although Calvin's intention was to make obedience to tyrants more acceptable, "the effect of his reasoning was to underscore the extraordinary nature of tyranny and to isolate it from the normal political relationship."[34]

Calvin and Social Contract

Calvin's attitude toward the idea of a social contract is ambivalent. Although Hearshaw is confident that Calvin "definitely excludes anything in the nature of a social contract,"[35] it is not to be so easily settled, for sometimes Calvin admits that "rulers owe responsibilities in turn to their subjects."[36] But the rulers' responsibility to their subjects in Calvin often has little practical import, since he parallels the nature of mutual responsibility between ruler and ruled to that between husband and wife or parents and children.

He reasons as follows: husbands and parents are bound to their wives and their children respectively by mutual responsibility. However, although "parents show themselves so hard and intractable to their children...that by their rigor they tire them beyond measure," and although "husbands most despitefully use their wives," the children and the wives "are still subject to their parents and husbands who are wicked and undutiful." Likewise, subjects are to obey wicked and unjust rulers.[37]

The problem with Calvin at this point is that he directly equates the nature of relationship between husband and wife or parents and children to that between ruler and ruled.[38] It is important to ask, however, whether the nature of mutual responsibility between ruler and ruled is exactly the same as that between parents and children or between husband and wife. Is this, for example, a biblical teaching?[39] In what ways ought rulers to undertake their responsibility to their subjects?

Calvin does not pay much attention to such questions. Instead, he simply insists that to vindicate the right is not the obligation of subjects, but of God: "the correction of unbridled despotism is the Lord's to avenge." We should not attempt to remedy tyranny. For us, "only this remains, to implore the Lord's help."[40]

Although Calvin was not an advocate of the absolute monarchy, arguing instead that the ideal form of government is "aristocracy, or a system compounded of aristocracy and democracy,"[41] he did not encourage the private citizens actively to participate in the politics.[42] "Under obedience," says Calvin, "I include the restraint which private citizens ought to bid themselves keep in public, that they may not deliberately intrude in public affairs, or pointlessly invade the magistrate's office, or undertake anything at all politically."[43]

What, then, is allowed for the private citizens to do for the amendment of public evils? According to Calvin, almost nothing is permitted except the petition: "If anything in a public ordinance requires amendment," says Calvin, instead of raising a tumult, or putting "their hands to the task," the citizenry ought to "commit the matter to the judgment of the magistrates...."[44] He was not an exponent of what is today called the participatory democracy.

Calvin keeps silent, however, about situations where the magistrates refuse amendment of the public evils for the sake of their own benefit. For the citizenry, Calvin was convinced, "to appeal to the conscience of the government" was "a proper protest" to the civil authority.[45] All they may rightly do is "to pray for deliverance, petition and remonstrate or take flight."[46]

The Biblical Ground of Obedience

The main source of Calvin's ideas on obedience to the political authority is the Scriptures. To support his arguments on this point,he quotes as many as forty biblical passages in the last chapter of his *Institutes.*

His argument for obedience to tyrants also is based on three passages in the Old Testament. Since Calvin's views on obedience are important to his political perspective, it will be helpful to look at his use of biblical examples in this regard.

His first example is that of Nebuchadnezzar in Jeremiah. In Jeremiah. 27: 5-8, 17, God pronounces:

> I have made the earth and men, says the Lord, and the anials which are upon the face of the earth, with my great and outstretched arm; and I give it to him who is pleasing in my eyes. Now, therefore, I have given all these lands into the hand of Nebuchadnezzar...my servant....all the nations and great kings shall serve him...until the time of his own land comes....And it shall be that any nation and kingdom that will not serve the king of Babylon, I shall visit the nation with sword, famine, and pestilence....Therefore, serve the king of Babylon and live.

Since it belongs to the sovereign "providence of God" to distribute kingdoms and appoint what kings he pleases, declares Calvin, "when we hear that a king has been ordained by God," we should "at once call to mind those heavenly edicts with regard to honoring and fearing a king." In other words, because "the Most High rules the kingdom of men, and gives it to whom he will" (Dan. 4:17), one's being on the throne is the only necessary and sufficient condition for subjects to pay full loyalty to him. The very fact that the Lord willed that unreserved obedience be rendered to "that abominable and cruel tyrant," Calvin goes on, demonstrates that "even the most worthless kings are appointed by the same decree by which the authority of all kings is established." [47]

Calvin seems to be straining to find biblical support for this contention. For example, was Nebuchadnezzar really a tyrant in the sense his argument requires? It is true that he was an "invader," a "conqueror" and even a "plunderer." But where does Calvin find the proof that Nebuchadnezzar practiced his kingship unrighteously and unjustly with regard to the internal affairs of his kingdom? Is it fair to label him as a "tyrant" because he was a pagan king and invader? Rather than generalizing the above command as imposed on all the people on earth groaning under tyranny, is it not more reasonable to view it as a unique command given specifically for the Israelites conquered by Nebuchadnezzar?

The second Scriptural passage Calvin interprets as teaching obedience to the tyrants is I Samuel 8:11-17:

> This shall be the right of the king that will reign over you: he will take your sons and put them to his chariot to make them his horsemen and to plow his fields and reap his harvest, and make his weapons. He will take your daughters to be perfumers and cooks and bakers. Finally, he will take your fields, your vineyards, and your best olive trees and will give them to his servants. He will take the tenth of your grain and of your vineyards, and will give it to his eunuchs and servants. He will take your menservants, maidservants, and asses and set them to his work. He will take the tenth of your flocks and you will be his servants.

Calvin sees this passage as in effect saying: "The willfulness of kings will run to excess, but it will not be your part to restrain it; you will have only this left to you: to obey their commands and hearken to their word."[48] But, once again, does the biblical text support Calvin's contention? Is this passage to be understood as inhibiting any action of subjects to restrain the tyranny? Is it not rather about the cost the Israelites would have to pay for the installment and maintenance of the monarchy, that is, the liability of tax payment, labor, and military service? If the above passage is a prediction that all the kings will be tyrants, how would he explain that there were some good kings in the history of Israel such as king David and Jehoshaphat? Furthermore, Calvin stressed previously that all rulers that exist are ordained by God. If so, does God always set up only tyrannical kings?

The third and last biblical passage on which Calvin bases his insistence on the obedience to the tyranny is the story of David and King

Saul. Calvin observes the statements of David in I Sam. 24:6 and 26:9-11, which were made while being persecuted by Saul:

> The Lord forbid that I should do this thing before the Lord, to my lord, the Lord's anointed, to put forth my hand against him, since he is the Lord's anointed. Who will put forth his hand against the anointed of the Lord and be innocent?...The Lord lives; unless the Lord strike him, or the day come for him to die, or he fall in battle, the Lord forbid that I should put forth my hand against the Lord's anointed.

Calvin's point is clear: as David regarded the life of his assailant as inviolable for the reason that God "sanctified" it, subjects also should not attempt to resist or depose tyrant. "It is not for us to remedy such evils." As all the kings are ordained by God, subjects should wait until God himself removes or deposes them. To subjects, "no command has been given except to obey and suffer."[49]

This point too is not without problems. First, Scripture does not describe king Saul as a tyrant who systematically oppressed the Israelite people and ruled unjustly over them. True, he failed to obey God at several critical moments, but Scripture does not depict his reign over his people as tyrannical. Secondly, it could be argued that the relationship between king Saul and David is a private one, concerned only with two individuals whereas the relation of the tyrant to the people is public one. David's refusal to kill Saul happened in the individual dimension. This cannot directly be applied to the public and collective relation between ruler and ruled.

If Calvin's understanding of these three passages is not based on a convincing interpretation of the texts, his point on obedience and non-resistance to the tyrant must also be viewed as highly questionable. But it is important to probe further into the underlying reasons for his formulations on this topic.

Passion for Order

There is a considerable scholarly agreement that the conservative bias in Calvin's political thought originates from his "passion for order."[50] In Calvin's view, fallen human nature is deeply depraved. The inordinate desires of that fallen nature pose a constant threat of total anarchy. In order to protect the society from this tumult and turbulence, there must be a repressive agent, i. e., a political ruler with power. Calvin's passion for order was so great that he came to think that for the sake of the cohesion and unity of the society the members of the society should be willing to accept any evil attended by the tyrants [51]: "No tyranny...can exist which does not in some respect assist in protecting the human society."[52] "There is much truth in the old saying that it is worse to live under a prince through whose lenity everything is lawful, than under a tyrant where there is no liberty at all."[53]

In addition to his innate passion for order, there was also a historical circumstance that led Calvin to call constantly for loyalty to the established authority. He wrote his chapter on civil government in the *Institute* within two years of the radical social experiments conducted by the Anabaptists, commended in such documents as the *Schleitheim Confession of Faith*.[54] Since Muenster, the suspicion that the Reformation might be a danger to the state made him very uneasy; he tried to keep a distance as far as possible from all revolutionary tendencies.[55] Thus, his conservative bias came to be reinforced by his contemporary political situation:

> ...whoever rises in rebellion against the magistrate, and those endowed with authority or official standing, is striving after anarchy. But a passion of that sort tends to be the disruption of order, yes, and what is more, deals a shattering blow to humanity itself.[56]

Church's Office of Watchman over the State

The preceding arguments constitute a very real "conservatism" in Calvin's view about political authority. But this is not the whole story for Calvin. Although the private citizens could do no more than to pray to God and appeal to the government for the amendment of the public ordinance, the church could and should do more than that.

Calvin thought one of the primary tasks of the church was to warn the authorities when they were at fault. Using an image from Ezekiel 3:17-18, he affirmed that the preachers were appointed in the church as "watchmen." All the teachers of the church, he declared, were "Divinely appointed and placed as on watch-towers, that they may keep watch for the common safety of all."[57] He considered that all rulers were subject to the preachers' criticism, made from the standpoint of scriptural religion.[58] The letter to Francis I of France which serves as an introduction to the *Institute* is just one of the many examples of Calvin's conviction that the dimension of "watchman" also belonged to the church's duty of proclamation.

Since God set the prophets and teachers "over nations and kingdoms" and put his words in their mouths (Jer. 1:9-10), Calvin contended, they might take courage and freely reprove kings and nations whenever it was needed.[59]

> The prophets...did not without reason direct their discourses to the chief men....as more guilt belongs always to leaders, this is the reason why the prophets treated them with more sharpness and severity...they who govern, pervert what is just and right, and then become the originators of all kinds of licentiousness. It is no wonder then that the Lord by his prophets inveighed so sharply against them.[60]

Magistrates of the People

At the end of his chapter on civil government, Calvin introduces some cases of exception in which the tyrannical ruler may be lawfully resisted. Among them, the penultimate paragraph of the *Institutes*, the "ephors" passage, is the most significant one for the later development of the restraining system of absolute monarchism. "So far, I have spoken only of private individuals," Calvin remarks as he signals a change of tone, however,

> if there are now any magistrates of the people, appointed to restrain the willfulness of kings (as in ancient times the ephors were set against the Spartan kings, or the tribunes of the people against the Roman consuls, or the demarches against the senate of the Athenians; and perhaps, as things now are, such power as the three estates exercise in every realm when they hold their chief assemblies), I am so far from forbidding them to withstand, in accordance with their duty, the fierce licentiousness of kings, that if they wink at kings who violently fall upon and assault the lowly common folk, I declare that their dissimulation involves nefarious perfidy, because they dishonestly betray the freedom of the people, of which they know that they have been appointed protectors by God's ordinance.[61]

In short, the constitutional defenders of the people's freedom may and should resist the wicked ruler. If not, they must be accused as the betrayers not only of people but of God, for they are both appointed by people ("*populares magistratus*") and ordained by God.[62]

Although this was no more than Calvin's reaffirmation of the already existing understanding of the role of the contemporary European quasi-representative organs,[63] it had an effect since in practice they were not at all performing their function of inviting them to play their original role. Suddenly, the office of the popular magistrates began to gain "a new dignity, a new spiritual strength."[64] The point was being made that they were "a rival agency" to the king, armed with a divine ordination, "the only credentials that most people of that period would respect."[65] Thus, the "ephors" passage provided "a balancing parallel" to Calvin's theory of obedience. The Pauline injunction of obedience to the political powers was still valid, but began to be understood as applying only to private citizens, not to popular magistrates.[66]

This "ephors" passage in the *Institutes* took on an important historical role in influencing later Calvinist political writers and revolutionaries in the sixteenth and seventeenth centuries.[67] As McNeill puts it, Calvin,

> unbarred the gate; a phalanx of champions of the people's rights against absolute and more or less tyrannical monarchs presently entered and ultimately stormed most of the bastions.[68]

In fact, this single dynamic sentence of 88 Latin words proved far more influential than his countless warnings against disobedience.[69] In the exigencies of the time, writers within the circle of Calvin's influence were led to seize upon the 'popular magistrate' passage. They emphasized and enlarged it all "out of proportion to what had been Calvin's dominant emphasis."[70] The "ephors" argument needed only the proper political context of armed conflict with the French king to develop into the powerful revolutionary ideology of Francis Hotman and Philip Mornay, "its animus against tyrants reaching in a secular form to the Estates General of 1789."[71] It also inspired some British seventeenth century political writers such as Rutherford, Sydney and Locke.

Logically, however, the "ephors" passage is not without problems. First, an inconsistency can be found in Calvin's understanding of the tyrant. As was observed previously, he maintained that the tyrants are a judgment of God for the sins of the people. Why, then, ought they to be checked by the ephoral magistrates? Is it not a vain attempt to block the implementation of divine providence? Or did Calvin consider that in the country where the ephoral magistrates exist, the tyrant's rule loses its religious meaning as a rod of God's wrath? Secondly, he does not mention the case where the ephoral magistrates "dissimulate" the arbitrary and licentious tyranny. What if they actually cooperate with the injustice of the ruler? What other challenges to tyrannical rule are permissible under such circumstances? Calvin is silent on these questions.

Obey God rather than Human

Calvin also suggests an exception to the rule of obedience for the private citizens. When kings "command anything against" God, claims Calvin, subjects need not pay attention to it.

> ...obedience [to the authority of rulers] is never to lead us away from obedience to him, to whose will the desires of all kings ought to be subject, to whose decrees all their commands ought to yield, to whose majesty their scepters ought to be submitted....[72] Whatever title then men may hold, they are to be listened to only on the condition that they do not lead us away from obeying God....We must obey princes and others who are in authority, but only in so far as they do not deny to God this rightful authority as the supreme king, Father, and Lord.[73]

This is to say, God places political authority over the people with a condition that he does not thereby impair His own authority. Therefore, they must obey the rulers in so far as the authority of God is not violated. Furthermore, when the rulers go so far as to violate God's honor, they are not to be regarded as authorities any longer. They are nothing. Here Calvin employs the logic of private-law theory:

> ...if a father, who is not content with his own station, tries to take from God the highest honor as Father, then he is a man and nothing else. If a king or prince or a magistrate extols himself so much that he minimizes the honor and authority of God, he is nothing but a man.[74]

It should be noted here that Calvin originally intended this exception to be applied primarily to religious matters, as is obvious when we examine the context in which this paragraph is located. Calvin is not talking about a situation where a prince rules tyrannically in general mundane affairs. Rather he is referring to a particular situation where the ruler directly commands people to do something against God, a situation where people cannot avoid choosing between obeying God's command and obeying the king's command. That Calvin had in mind primarily ritual and worship is confirmed by the fact that he suggests as a prototype of proper Christian disobedience the case of Daniel, who refused to obey the "impious" edict of Darius (Dan. 6:22-23). Therefore, we can safely conclude that in the last paragraph of the *Institutes* Calvin intended to authorize disobedience by the private citizens to the civil authority in a very limited and specific case directly related to the cult, such as when the king commands people to worship the pagan gods.

Later Calvinists raised questions about this line of argument. Does God's will only apply to cultic beliefs and practices? Does not God's will encompass other areas of human life? Does God have something to say only in the church? In the judgment of some later Calvinists, it was out of character for Calvin to operate with a narrow understanding of these issues, since he insisted elsewhere that God's purposes apply to every realm of human life. As Calvin regularly taught, God wanted the universe to be arranged according to his "order."

The problem with Calvin's treatment of political obedience, then, is that the ruler's will frequently conflicted with God's, although it was not necessarily concerning the cult.[75] In this case, what are believers supposed to do? Does Calvin's rule of exception apply to these cases too? It did not take so long for later Calvinists to draw an answer: whether Calvin implied it or not in his last paragraph of the *Institutes*, a human authority which contradicts divine will, no matter what it may concern, should be disobeyed and even resisted. Hearshaw puts the point in this way:

> The reservation which Calvin made to his doctrine of obedience, that we must obey God rather than men, cannot easily be confined...to the question of worship. It may be that God has commands other than those concerning cult and church, and that in the state itself the maxim applies.[76]

Furthermore, once God's will is known, faithfulness requires the believer to obey it. The rule of exception which Calvin intended to be applied to religious matters, thus, began to be applied extensively and intensively to all the mundane matters. In this way Calvinism contributed to the restraining of absolute monarchism.

No More than Passive Resistance

It must be emphasized here, however, that Calvin is not giving or implying, in any of his comments on disobedience, a sanction to active resistance against human authority. What he authorizes is no more than passive resistance:

> I know with what great and present peril this constancy is menaced, because kings bear defiance with the greatest displeasure, whose "wrath is a messenger of death"(Prov. 16:14), says Solomon.... let us comfort ourselves with the thought that we are rendering that obedience which the Lord requires when we *suffer anything* rather than turn aside from piety [my italics].[77]

When the king's command creates a conflict with God's, Calvin does not hesitate to recommend resistance to the king. That resistance, however, "always stops just short of organized rebellion and revolution."[78] Indeed, he "carefully guards against any endorsement of popular revolutionary action."[79] In 1554, when John Knox wrote a letter to Calvin asking whether it is permitted for the nobles or inferior magistrates "who are still in military occupation of towns and fortresses" to resist "a Magistrate who enforces idolatry and condemns true religion," Calvin wrote to Bullinger that he had answered "the Scot" that "under no circumstances" is active resistance justifiable.[80] In 1560, Calvin said to a Huguenot leader who had asked his opinion about their conspiracy of rebellion that he was not satisfied "unless they should be perfectly on their guard not to shed blood," for he believed "it to be an inevitable consequence that from a single drop would immediately flow streams that would inundate France."[81] This explains at least in part why the first Calvinists often chose such individual responses to persecution as quick martyrdom or flight from their homeland.

Veering toward Active Resistance

Although Skinner argues that "until the closing years of his life," Calvin remained a staunch advocate of "absolute non-resistance,"[82] there are signs that near the end of his life, Calvin began to modify his doctrine of passive obedience.[83] Perhaps influenced by the success of John Knox in Scotland and by Beza's tract,[84] he began to veer toward an acceptance of active resistance. He also began to have sympathy for the argument that the coronation oaths and the laws of a country formed a system of agreements which might be defended against an arbitrary ruler.[85]

Since we will be looking at how Calvinism can be adapted for new historical circumstances, it will be helpful to offer a brief case study in this chapter as to how Calvin himself interacted with historical events. Some historical knowledge of the conspiracy of Amboise is needed to understand the background of Calvin's change in his view of resistance.[86]

In July 1559, King Henry of France was seriously wounded during a tournament by a lance that penetrated his eye. A few days later he died of his injuries and was succeeded by his teenage son Francis II, husband of Mary, Queen of Scots. The staunchly Catholic faction of the Guises from Lorraine immediately took over most of the functions of the government for the young and sickly king. Persecutions of the Huguenots soon increased, and whatever influence Anthony of Navarre as the first prince of the blood and his brother Louis de Conde still had on the king and the Queen mother was more and more deterred.

In the fall of 1559, a conspiracy sprouted, probably in the mind of a young nobleman by the name of La Renaudie. He seems to have planned to organize a surprise attack on the French court while it was assembled at Amboise, kidnap the person of the young king, assassinate the Guise regents, and place France under Bourbon control, that is, under the leadership of Anthony of Navarre and Conde. La Renaudie went to Geneva to seek the approval of Calvin. Referring to his interview with La Renaudie, Calvin wrote later in a letter to the Admiral de Coligny that he "adopted so decided a tone in condemning all his proposals." Nevertheless, La Renaudie went ahead with his plan and carried it out in March, 1560. But the Guises apparently were expecting it; the conspirators were overpowered and most of them were killed including La Renaudie.[87]

What is remarkable concerning this incident is the fact that during the interview with La Renaudie, Calvin hinted at his first approval of armed resistance, albeit with qualifications. "I admitted, it is true," writes Calvin in the same letter, "that if the princes of the blood demanded to be maintained in their rights for the common good, and if the Parliament joined them in their quarrel, that it would then be lawful for all good subjects to lend them armed assistance."[88]

In January 1562, Charles IX signed an edict that went quite far in the direction of tolerance. Protestant worship was allowed anywhere except within city-boundaries and the king as well as the Queen Mother was obliged to maintain the edict. The Protestants started to exercise these new rights without any hesitation. But the Duke of Guise, who was infuriated by this new development, took an action against the Protestants. In March, he and his horsemen came upon a worshipping community of Huguenots at Vassey and massacred about seventy people. The Edict of January had been violated in direct opposition to the king and the Queen Mother.

At this time, Calvin was convinced that armed resistance was not illegitimate, for positive law had been broken. Setting out to organize military campaigns, he wrote to Sturm in Strasbourg immediately after the massacre of Vassey that "to repress their [the Guises'] assaults it is of the highest importance that the princes of Germany should interfere to exhort the king to constancy, and declare that their good offices will be employed in his favor as far as opportunities will permit."[89] In June, he wrote to the Bailiff of Lausanne urging "the speedy dispatch of the succors" from such Swiss cantons as Bern, Valais and Neuchatel to the Reformed who were besieged in Lyons.[90]

To Calvin's disappointment, however, the auxiliaries he expected from Germany did not arrive and the Bernese were slow in response. He wrote to Bullinger in August stressing that the Bernese troops "should march straight to join the prince of Conde...." His tone sounds unusually desperate:

> If you perceive that your authority can have any influence in eciding the senate of Berne to permit their troops to join the prince, I entreat you to strain every nerve for that purpose, because if war is protracted any longer, we are completely ruined, as well as the kingdom.[91]

Even to the churches that he had earlier exhorted to suffer and submit, Calvin addressed an appeal for the liberal provision for the expenses of the war:

> I trust that the thing itself being properly understood by you will suffice to touch your hearts to devote yourselves to the good cause without reserve, each according to his means. The point in question is to find money to support the troops....God has reduced us to such an extremity that if you are not succored from that quarter, we can expect nothing, according to human probability, but a pitiful and horrible desolation.[92]

The Protestants were greatly disheartened when Conde was captured by the enemy and on March 12, 1563, signed the Peace of Amboise under pressure and for his recovery of liberty. As a consequence some grave restrictions were introduced into the Edict of January. Calvin did not give up all hope, however, and tried to exhort Conde to go on in armed resistance for the consolidation of whatever freedom still remained:

> Experience has already proved to you how audaciously the enemies of God undertake to do evil, unless they be *vigorously resisted*....It is at this moment that you should labor more than ever, since God seems to be holding out his hand to you, and as he has done you the inestimable honor of charging you to *maintain his quarrel with your sword*....[my italics][93]

Some argue that in those letters Calvin encouraged armed resistance not against "the establish order, but against a rebellion to that order," for the Guises "violated the edicts of the highest power in the state, the king." This is to say that even during the trying last few years of his life, Calvin remained absolutely faithful to his earlier position of forbidding active resistance to the ruler.[94]

It is true that Calvin strived to remain faithful to the laws of the country to a remarkable extent. But it would be misleading to insist that he retained "absolute faithfulness" to his earlier principle. For if the Guises violated the positive law, to remedy that evil was primarily the responsibility of the king and the government, not of the individual nobility such as Conde. The first responsibility of maintaining the social order against the violators was not to be imposed upon a few noblemen setting aside the sovereign ruler and his government. If Calvin had been "absolutely" faithful to his principle, he would have left the punishment of the Guises to the hands of the king instead of inciting Conde to rise with force.

It does seem undeniable that Calvin had become much more radical on the subject of resistance in his last years. Several paragraphs of Calvin written in this period demonstrated his change. In the second edition of *Commentary on Acts* published in 1560, he writes:

> ...as soon as governors lead us away from obedience to God, seeing that they enter into conflict with God impiously and boldly, they *must be put in their place*...Then all the fumes of their offices will vanish....anyone who goes beyond his function, because he sets himself against God, *must be stripped of the title of his office*.[95]

In the *Commentary on Daniel* 6:22 published in 1561, his language is far less guarded:

> For earthly princes lay aside their power when they rise up against God, and are unworthy of being reckoned in the number of mankind. We ought rather utterly to defy [*conspuere in ipsorum capita*, literally, "to spit on their heads"] than to obey them....[96]

It is notable, however, that, as was mentioned above, Calvin's sanction of resistance to the tyrant was always a qualified one: it had to be led by the "princes of the blood" or the parliament. One year prior to his death, Calvin was still insisting on the necessity of the legal right to take the initiative to active resistance. At least consciously, he did not authorize private citizens to do so. To a nobleman who, dissatisfied with the Treaty of Amboise, was tempted to revolt, he wrote: "I do not see by what title you could do so, since God has disarmed you....to attempt anything, unless we be called and warranted to do so, can never come to any good." Calvin's advice for him was to "stick to the saying of Abraham, 'God will provide for the matter,' as indeed the apostle reminds us that 'he is faithful, and thus will not suffer us to be tempted above what we can bear.'"[97]

Open Avenger

Interestingly, however, there is one passage in the *Institutes* where Calvin was unconsciously justifying active resistance to the tyrants by a private citizen. As we already observed, he suggested that the only thing that private individuals can do under tyranny is to pray to God for delivery. How, then, does God answer such prayer? How does God vindicate the right of subjects? "Sometimes," Calvin answers, "he raises up open avengers from among his servants and arms them with his command to punish the wicked government and deliver his people, oppressed in unjust ways, from miserable calamity." In this case, "taking up arms against kings" does "not at all violate that majesty...implanted in kings by God's ordination."[98]

This is, in effect, a release of permission for prospective revolutionary leaders. For if violent resistance is allowed for those who receive "God's lawful calling" for revolution, how is it possible in any other way than through one's being convicted of its necessity and imperativeness? Calvin would not suggest that God's calling for it is delivered through such mystical channels as dreams, visions, or God's voice. How, then, is the legitimacy of a revolution to be discerned except by its success? As Michael Waltzer argues, by this passage "Calvin had merely readmitted the tyrannicide under the cover of divinity. In so doing, he revealed that the legitimacy of resistance was at least in part a *post facto* ascription."[99]

Conclusion

Some people argue that Calvin, "through temperament and teaching," established "his credentials as a conservative."[100] Such an evaluation might be valid only so far as his resistance theory is concerned. In the consideration of "order," he was very cautious in issuing permission for popular revolution.

We must be aware, however, that his conservatism was never of such a kind as to argue that Christians have nothing to do with politics. As John T. McNeill states, Calvin would be "repelled and even appalled by the type of sectarian spirituality that would desert the sphere of politics as beneath the spiritual man's plane of living."[101] Or in Hopfl's phrase, "Calvin did not believe that political and religious matters are ultimately separable....he could not possibly be thought to have regarded civil laws and institutions as matters remote from theology...."[102]

Nor did Calvin think that the churches should keep silent on the socio-political issues. Rather, Calvin and his fellow pastors were so active in pronouncing the opinion of the church concerning the contemporary political issues that sometimes it seemed that in Calvin's Geneva the distinction between church and state tended to blur.[103] The clergy spoke to the state as a church because they thought themselves to be the "mouth of God" with the duty of speaking out sharply against all injustices by the government. To them, church and state were unquestionably under the Lordship of Christ.

In showing concern for contemporary political issues, Calvin was second to none. A Calvin scholar writes that "it would be difficult or impossible to name another eminent theologian whose correspondence is so fraught with references to contemporary political issues."[104] For this reason, a historian of political ideas could write that "In the history of political thought in the sixteenth century, there was no agent of more importance than was Jean Calvin."[105] Since he was so eager to see the will of God extend to the total community, he regarded so many problems as religious that another age might consider political. "He was an almost thoroughgoing secularist in the sense that he understood the gospel to be irrevocably concerned with the world."[106]

Unlike some modern conservative Christians, Calvin considered that the discussion on civil government should occupy one chapter in his *Institutes on Christian Religion.* He never thought that theology was one thing, and politics was another. Thus his "ephors" passage alongside his principle that Christians should obey God rather than man exerted a profound influence on the development of the later Calvinists' theory of resistance.

In discussing Calvin's political ideas, we do need to take into account the sixteenth-century context of his thoughts. Nonetheless, as Ronald VanderMolen has argued, a proper historical understanding of early Calvinism can provide a background for developing a Christian perspective within a twentieth-century milieu without rejecting Calvin's ideal as based on Jewish and medieval cultural models.[107]

Before looking at how these theses can be applied to a twentieth century setting, we will examine in closer detail how Calvin's views were developed and re-contextualized by some of his younger disciples.

1 The following discussion on the background of Calvin's rediscovery of the value of politics is largely based on Sheldon S. Wolin's insightful work, Politics and Vision: Continuity and Innovation in Western Political Thought (Boston, 1960), esp. Ch. 6, "Calvin: The Political Education of Protestantism."

2 In his commentary on Romans 13:1, Calvin draws an analogy between the restless spirit of a group of the first century Christians and the Anabaptists of his own day, though he singles out no group by name. He describes some early Christians to have considered that in order to enjoy Christian liberty they should shake off "every yoke of human slavery" and that Christ's Kingdom can be established only after abolishing all the earthly powers. Calvin, *Commentary on the Epistles of Paul the Apostle to the Romans and to the Thessalonians*, eds. David W. Torrance and Thomas F. Torrance, trans. Ross Mackenzie (Grand Rapids, Michigan: Eerdmans, 1961), 280-281.

3 Calvin, *Institutes of the Christian Religion*, ed. John McNeill, trans. Ford L. Battles (Philadelphia, 1960), IV, xx, 1.

4 *Ibid.*, IV, xx, 2.

5 Wolin, *Politics and Vision*, 168.

6 *Institutes,* IV, xx, 2.

7 John T. McNeill, "The Democratic Element in Calvin's Thought," *Church History* 18 (1949): 155.

8 McNeill, "Calvin and Civil Government," in Donald K. McKim ed., *Readings in Calvin's Theology* (Grand Rapids, Michigan: Baker Book House, 1984), 262.

9 For an excellent discussion of Calvin's rigorous involvement in all the areas of life in Geneva such as politics, economics, society, etc...see, Fred Graham, *The Constructive Revolutionary John Calvin and His Socio-Economic Impact* (Michigan State University Press, 1987).

10 Calvin begins his chapter on civil government with an idea similar to the "two kingdom" theory of Luther: Christians are living under the "twofold government." One "resides in the soul or inner man," and "pertains to eternal life." The other deals with "civil justice and outward morality." *Institutes*, IV, xx, 1.

11 Here Calvin has in mind the Anabaptists whom he criticized as "insane and barbarous," for, he writes, "in unbridled license" they

were striving to overturn the "divinely established order" of civil government. *Institutes,* IV, xx, 1, 2.

12 *Institutes*, IV, xx, 2, 3.

13 Luther thought that what can reasonably be required of the government was the protection of the society from the expressions of evil human nature and the preservation of the liberty of the church to proclaim the gospel.

14 *Institutes*, IV, xx, 4.

15 Calvin, *Commentary on Rom.* 13:3. Calvin, however, does not deny here that the government has, as a part of its duty, the function of restraining "the waywardness" of "the public enemies of human race" for the protection of the society from "universal destruction."

16 *Institutes*, IV, xx, 3.

17 *Corpus Reformatorum,* 55, 559, quoted in David Little, *Religion, Order and Law* (The University of Chicago Press, 1984), 44. Subsequent references to this work will be using the abbreviation "CR."

18 Calvin, *Comm. on Rom.* 13:1.

19 *Institutes*, IV, xx, 4, 22.

20 *Institutes*, IV, xx, 22.

21 Comm. Rom. 13:2; *Institutes* IV, xx, 23.

22 *Institutes*, IV, xx, 25.

23 Calvin, *Sermons on the Epistles to Timothy and Titus* (Edinburgh: The Banner of Truth Trust, 1983), 1206.

24 Comm. Rom.13:1; *Institute*, IV, xx, 28.

25 William A. Mueller, *Church and State in Luther and Calvin* (Nashville, Tennessee: Broadman Press, 1954), 133.

26 F. J. C. Hearshaw, *The Social and Political Ideas of Some Great Thinkers of the Renaissance and the Reformation* (London, 1925), 213.

27 In his commentary on Rom. 13:1-7, however, Calvin recognizes that there is inherent limitation in the power of the rulers. As Rom. 13:4 says that rulers are God's servants to do subjects good, asserts Calvin, their power is "restricted to the welfare of their subjects." cf. David C. Steinmetz, "Calvin and Melanchthon on Romans 13:1-7," *Ex Auditu* (Princeton Theological Seminary, 1986), 74-81.

[28] *Institutes*, IV, xx, 29, 25, 26, 30, 27.

[29] *Institutes*, IV, xx, 29, 27.

[30] Thomas Aquinas argued that if the ruler is a usurper, there is no moral obligation at all for subjects to obey him. Moreover, he justified tyrannicide when the tyrant's title was defective. He asserted that if a legitimate ruler exceeds his authority but commands what is not sinful, subjects are morally free to obey him or not, as they choose. For Aquinas's view on this subject, see *Summa Theologiae* I-II, 6. 4; I-II 97; II-II, 104. 6. ad 3; II-II. 42. 2. ad 3 and *On Kingship, to the King of Cyprus*, a translation and revision of Aquinas' work, *De Regno, ad regnem Cypri* by Gerald B. Phelan and I. Th. Eschmann (Toronto: Pontifical Institute of Medieval Studies, 1949), i-6-44, 46, 49, 50, 51, 52 and Aquinas, *The Commentary on the Sentences of Peter Lombard,* II sent. 44. 2.

[31] Harro Hopfl, *The Christian Polity of John Calvin* (Cambridge University Press, 1982), 49.

[32] *Institutes*, IV, xx, 25.

[33] *Institutes*, IV, xx, 29.

[34] Wolin, *Politics and Vision*, 187.

[35] Hearshaw, *The Social and Political Ideas*, 213.

[36] *Institutes*, IV, xx, 29.

[37] *Institutes*, IV, xx, 29.

[38] William Bouwsma observes in Calvin a "deep attachment to a traditional paternalistic model of politics." For Calvin, he notes, there was a "paternal chain" that connects God the Father, the spiritual fathers, and the father of his country or his city fathers. William Bouwsma, *John Calvin: A Sixteenth-Century Portrait* (Oxford University Press, 1988), 211.

[39] In chapters 5-6 of Ephesians where Paul teaches about the mutual responsibilities among human beings, he does not make any mention of the relationship between ruler and ruled.

[40] *Institutes*, IV, xx, 31, 29.

[41] *Institutes*, IV, xx, 8.

[42] Michael Waltzer should have distinguished Calvin's attitude from later Calvinists' toward the ordinary people's participation in the politics. It may be true that later Calvinists "taught previously passive

men the styles and method of political activity and enabled them successfully to claim the right of participation" in the politics. Michael Waltzer, *Revolution of the Saints* (Harvard University Press, 1965), 18. However, it is difficult to find in the writings of Calvin such positive statements concerning the common people's political involvement. For this very reason, Marc-Edouard Cheneviere declares that Beza, Hotman, Mornay, William of Orange, Buchanan, Althusius, and Roger Williams are not orthodox Calvinists, and that to the extent that they defended the liberal and democratic ideas they merely developed ideas that had already existed before the Reformation. Edouard Cheneviere *La pensee politique de Calvin* (Geneva, 1937), 10-12.

43 *Institutes,* IV, xx, 23.

44 *Institutes*, IV, xx, 23.

45 Willem Balke, *Calvin and the Anabaptist Radicals*, trans. William Heynen (Grand Rapids, Michigan, 1981), 292.

46 Hoepfl, *The Christian Polity*, 49.

47 *Institutes,* IV, xx, 26, 27.

48 *Institutes*, IV, xx, 26.

49 *Institutes,* IV, xx, 28, 29, 31.

50 This suggestive term is the translation by David Little of Josef Bohatec's phrase in *Calvin und das Recht* (Vienna, 1934), 62, quoted in Little, *Religion*, 42.

51 Wolin, *Politics and Vision*, 186.

52 Comm. Rom. 13:3.

53 Calvin, *Commentary on the Book of Psalms*, trans. James Anderson, (Grand Rapids, Michigan: Wm. B. Eerdmans, 1963), 3: 106.

54 Quentin Skinner, *The Foundations of Modern Political Thought* (Cambridge University Press, 1988), 193.

55 Willem Balke, *Calvin and the Anabaptist Radicals*, 290.

56 Calvin, *Commentary on the Acts of the Apostles,* trans. John W. Fraser (Grand Rapids, Michigan, 1973), 2: 229-230.

57 Calvin, *Commentaries on the First Twenty Chapters of the Book of the Prophet Ezekiel,* trans., Thomas Myers, (Grand Rapids, Michigan, Wm. B. Eerdmans), 1:148-149.

58 *Institutes*, IV,xx, 6. For the discussion of the church's office of watchman over the state, see, Eberhard Busch, "Church and Politics in the Reformed Tradition," in James E. Bradley and Richard A. Muller, eds. *Church, Word, and Spirit* (Grand Rapids, Michigan, 1987), 172-176; John McNeill, "Calvin and Civil Government," in McKim, ed. *Readings,* 262.

59 Calvin, *Commentaries on the Book of the Prophet Jeremiah*, trans. and ed. John Owen, (Grand Rapids, Michigan, Wm. B. Eerdmans, 1950), 1:44.

60 Calvin, *Commentaries on the Twelve Minor Prophets*, trans. John Owen, (Grand Rapids, Michigan), vol. 2, *Joel, Amos, Obadiah*, 363-364.

61 *Institutes*, IV, xx, 31. Elsewhere Calvin expands on this point: "...certain remedies against tyranny are allowable, for example, when magistrates and estates have been constituted and given the care of the commonwealth: they shall have power to *keep the prince to his duty* and even to *coerce* him if he attempt anything unlawful" [my Italics]. *Opera Omnia*, ed. Baum et al., vol. 29, 557, 636-637, 238-9, quoted in Wolin, *Vision*, 188.

62 Concerning the source of the authority for the popular magistrates to resist the tyrant, there exist conflicting interpretations among scholars. H. A. Lloyd sees Roman law as a source of Calvin's thought. By indicating the fact that in Roman law the guardian did not derive his authority from the ward, but from the law, or decree of the senate, or the emperor himself, he argues that Calvin had "no intention of arguing for a democratic case. The popular magistrates were not elected by their ward, the people, and they were not responsible to the latter. They were appointed, and by the only authority competent to do so—namely, God himself." H. A. Lloyd, "Calvin and the Duty of Guardians to Resist," *Journal of Ecclesiastical History*, vol. 32, No. 1 (Jan. 1981): 65-67.

Waltzer also argues that "Calvin never imagined officers or nobles as representatives....particular officers were created only by God....Resistance was thus not a representative but a conscientious act, public not in a secular but in a religious sense. Magistrates were morally (not civilly) guilty if they failed to resist a tyrant." Waltzer, *The Revolution*, 60.

On the contrary, John McNeill affirms that Calvin "was doubtless aware that the classes of ancient magistrates here mentioned were all elected by popular vote. This was uniformly the case in the membership of the estates...." McNeill, "Calvin and Civil Government," *Readings,* McKim, ed. 269.

Skinner's view seems balanced in being inclusive of both: he asserts that the popular magistrates discussed by Calvin are "clearly regarded not simply as ordained powers, but also as elected officials...." Skinner, *The Foundations,* 233-4. Most probably, Calvin thought that God ordained the popular magistrates through the procedure of popular election.

63 Calvin must have been aware that the French estates had not even met since three years before his own birth.

64 Hans Baron, "Calvinist Republicanism and Its Historical Roots," *Church History* 8 (1939): 36.

65 Wolin, *Politics and Vision*, 188.

66 R. M. Kingdon, "The Political Resistance of the Calvinists in France and the Low Countries," *Church History* 27 (1958): 227.

67 Skinner seems to disagree on this point, arguing that because of the "circumspection" of his language, Calvin at first had exercised "little influence." Skinner points out that "there is no reference to ephoral magistrates in the political writings of Beza or [Peter] Martyr...nor is the idea even mentioned even in the most revolutionary writings of Knox and Goodman at the end of the decade." Ultimately, however, he does not deny that Calvin's analysis made "an important contribution to the stock of radical political ideas available to his followers" by introducing "a secular and constitutional element" into the discussion of political authority. Skinner, *The Foundations*, 233.

68 McNeill, "The Democratic Element," 163.

69 McNeill, "John Calvin on Civil Government," in George L. Hunter, ed., *Calvinism and the Political Order* (Philadelphia, 1964), 40.

70 Keith L. Griffin, "Reluctant Revolutionaries: The Middle Colony Reformed Idea of a Just Resistance," Ph. D. diss., Fuller Theological Seminary, 1989.

[71] Lowell H. Zuck, ed., *Christianity and Revolution: Radical Christian Testimonies, 1520-1650* (Philadelphia: Temple University Press, 1975), 139.

[72] *Institutes*, IV, xx, 32.

[73] Comm. Acts 4: 19.

[74] Comm. Acts 5:29.

[75] Richard Mouw describes this divine-human will conflict as the "weightier will" argument. Richard Mouw, *The God Who Commands* (Notre Dame, Indiana: Notre Dame University Press, 1990), 98-9.

[76] Hearshaw, *The Social and Political Ideas*, 215.

[77] *Institutes,* IV, xx, 32.

[78] Clarence J. Vos, "Human Authority: A Biblical Study with a Comparison of Calvin's view," in David E. Holwerda, ed. *Exploring the Heritage of John Calvin* (Grand Rapids, Michigan, 1976), 228.

[79] McNeill, footnote 54 on *Institutes*, IV, xx, 31.

[80] Richard L. Greaves, *Theology and Revolution in the Scottish Revolution: Studies in the Thought of John Knox* (Grand Rapids, Michigan, 1980), 128; Jasper Ridley, *John Knox* (Oxford University Press, 1968), 179.

[81] Letter to Peter Martyr, May 11, 1560, in Julet Bonnet, ed., *Letters of John Calvin* (New York, 1972), 4:107.

[82] Skinner, *The Foundations*, 193.

[83] It is interesting to observe that Luther also passed through a serious change in his view of resistance to the emperor. He underwent three stages of slow but radical transition: first, the period down to 1530, when he opposed resistance to the emperor under all circumstances; secondly, the period after the declaration of Torgau in 1530, when he conceded with extreme reluctance that there might possibly be a valid legal right of resistance; finally, a period at the end of his life, when he reversed many of his earlier views and emerged as an outspoken champion of resistance to the emperor. For more detail, see, Manfred Hoffman, "Martin Luther: Resistance to Secular Authority," *The Journal of International Theological Center* 12 (Fall 1984/Spring 1985): 35-49; W. D. J. Cargill Thompson, "Luther and the Right of Resistance to the Emperor," *Church, Society and Politics* (1975), 159-202.

[84] Robert M. Kingdon has suggested the possibility that Beza, when he adopted a radical political stance in his tract *The Punishment of Heretics by the Civil Magistrate* (1554), may, in turn, have had an influence on Calvin himself. Kingdon, "The First Expression of Theodore Beza's Political Ideas", *Archiv fur R eformationsgeschichte* 46 (1955), 95.

[85] Wolin asserts that Calvin was very sensitive to the "plurality of relationships," that is, the "triangular relationship" of ruler, people, and the law. For Calvin, he says, the connecting link between ruler and subjects was the law. It had the effect of adding one more obligatory element to the ruler's office besides his responsibilities to God and the people. The sum total of these obligations provided "a possibility of resistance" for the Calvinists. Wolin, *Politics and Vision*, 188.

[86] The outline given here of the Conspiracy of Amboise is based on the account of Robert M. Kingdon, *Geneva and the Coming of the Wars of Religion in France, 1555-1563* (Geneva: Librairie E. Droz, 1956), 68-76.

[87] For more detailed study of the intricacies of this plot, see, N. Sutherland, "Calvinism and the Conspiracy of Amboise," *History* 47 (1962): 111-38.

[88] Letter to the Admiral de Coligny, April 16, 1561, Bonnet, 4: 176-7. In offering this and the following accounts, I am relying to some degree on the studies of these events by Christoph Jungen, "Calvin and the Origin of political Resistance Theory in the Calvinist Tradition," Th. M. Thesis, Westminster Theological Seminary, 1980, 110-138.

[89] Letter to Sturm, Mar. 25, 1562, Bonnet, 4:269.

[90] Letter to Monsieur de Diesbach, June 13, 1562, Bonnet, 4:274.

[91] Letter to Bullinger, Aug. 15, 1562, Bonnet, 4:275ff.

[92] Letter to the Churches of Languedoc, Sep., 1562 (without a date), Bonnet, 4:278.

[93] Letter to Conde, May 10, 1563, Bonnet, 4:309ff.

[94] Jungen, "Calvin and the Origin of Political Resistance Theory," 137-138.

[95] comm. Acts 5:29.

[96] Calvin, *Commentaries on the Book of the Prophet Daniel*, trans. Thomas Myers, (Grand Rapids, Michigan: Wm. B. Eerdmans Publishing Co., 1948), 382.

[97] Letter to Soubise, May 25, 1563. Bonnet, 4:317.

[98] *Institutes*, IV, xx, 30.

[99] Waltzer, *The Revolution*, 63.

[100] Norman F. Langford, "Christians and Politics," *Church and Society* 62 (1972):12.

[101] McNeill, "Calvin and Civil Government," 261.

[102] Harro Hopfl, *The Christian Polity of John Calvin*, 149.

[103] Bouwsma, *John Calvin*, 210.

[104] McNeill, "John Calvin on Civil Government," 24.

[105] J. W. Allen, *A History of Political Thought in the Sixteenth Century*, 2nd ed. (London: Methuen & Co., Ltd, 1961), 49.

[106] Graham, *The Constructive Revolutionary*, 160-161.

[107] Ronald VanderMolen, "Political Calvinism," *Journal of Church and State* 11 (1969): 463.

CHAPTER II

KNOX AND BEZA ON RESISTANCE TO POLITICAL AUTHORITY

Scholars commonly claim that a distinction should be made between the political thought of John Calvin and that of his followers. They argue that it is especially important to make this distinction with reference to resistance theories. For example, Ronald VanderMolen asserts that "There is a definite difference between the political Calvin and the political Calvinists, a difference forced by historical circumstances." Calvin's followers "altered Calvin's view of resistance as new circumstances dictated...[T]he new Calvinist formulated a new politics of revolution...."[1] J.W.Allen states that Theodore Beza's essay, *De jure Magistratuum*, was "in flat contradiction of his master's teaching." He also insists that John Knox must be regarded as "one of the chief personal factors in the history of political thought in the sixteenth century," because he played such an important part in the "repudiation by Calvinists of one of the essential points of Calvin's teaching."[2]And Richard L. Greaves contends that "Knox's assertion of rebellion was... a revolutionary departure from the views propounded by Calvin prior to 1560."[3]

Is this really so? To what extent are these arguments based on an accurate assessment of developments within Calvinism? To answer these questions we need to examine the political writings of the second generation Calvinists, and then compare them with Calvin's. This chapter will analyze the political documents of John Knox and Theodore Beza, the two foremost Calvinist Reformers, with special reference to their theory of resistance to the unjust secular powers.

John Knox and His Resistance Theory

As was the case with most of the Reformers, Knox's resistance theory developed by degrees. He started as a typical political conservative following the line of Tyndale, who represented the traditional English view of the temporal powers.[4] A letter written by Knox in 1552 reflects this. Writing to his congregation of Berwick, he exhorts them to obey the king and the magistrates, no matter "how ungodly that ever their precepts or commandments be." The only case where disobedience was justified was when "a chief point of religion" was violated. Even then, he adds, armed resistance was not acceptable. They were "not to pretend to defend God's truth or religion by violence or sword." Instead, they were to suffer patiently "what God shall please be laid upon you for constant confession of your faith and belief."[5]

Our political outlook is most likely to be influenced by the age we are living in. Knox was no exception in this respect. His passive attitude began to change after Mary's accession to the throne in 1553. Radicalism is, at times, a reaction to persecution. If only Mary had tolerated Protestant worship in England, Knox would have remained a political conservative. By the time Knox wrote his first treatise, *A Confession and Declaration of Prayers* (written within a few weeks of Mary's victory), Protestant congregations could still meet in safety and the mass was not yet restored. Accordingly, nothing appeared in the *Confession* that could be held to be seditious. Even his warning against the danger of a return to popery had been hidden in the form of a prayer for the Queen.[6] As Mary's attempt to restore Catholicism intensified, however, Knox's writings got more and more radical.

Knox first introduces a resistance theme, though somewhat vaguely, in *A Godly Letter of Warning or Admonition to the Faithful in London, New Castle and Berwick*. He started writing this epistle in December 1553 in London and completed it in January 1554 at Dieppe. The central message of this letter was that the Protestants should not attend the Catholic mass. "The end of my admonition is," said Knox, "that even as you purpose and intend to avoid God's vengeance, both in this life and in the life to come; that so you avoid and fly, as well in body as in spirit, all fellowship and society with idolaters in their idolatry."[7] The maximum Knox required of believers was separation from evil.

In this letter, Knox introduces his vital idea of covenant for the first time. Scholars agree that the covenant concept was the very foundation on which Knox built up his resistance theory.[8] He defines the covenant as:

> the league between God and us, that he alone shall be our God, and we shall be his people. He shall communicate with us of his graces and goodness: We

> shall serve him in body and spirit. He shall be our safe guard from death and damnation. We shall seek to him, and shall fly from all strange gods. In making this league, solemnly we swear never to have fellowship with one religion, except with that which God has confirmed by his manifest Word.[9]

Knox argues that because of this covenant between God and the people, the English Protestants are not to be conformed to Roman Catholicism. "Why is it necessary that we avoid idolatry?" argues Knox, "because that otherwise we declare ourselves little to regard the league and covenant of God...."[10] As Reid put it, since the Englishmen accepted "the true religion," England became a "covenanted country." For that reason, to go back to Catholicism was taken as breaking the covenant.[11]

In order to discharge the covenant obligation, mere avoidance of attending the Roman Mass was not enough. Something positive was required of them: an open and outward declaration of their hostility toward the idolaters. "All those that would draw us from God (be they kings or queens)," says Knox, "being of devil's nature, are enemies unto God, and therefore will God that in such cases we declare ourselves enemies unto them."[12] In asking his congregations to denounce Roman Catholicism openly, Knox was apparently going beyond the boundary of passive disobedience.

In some places in the *Letter*, Knox expresses even more radical sentiments. It would not even be unfair to take Knox to be insisting on the execution of all the Catholics when he argues that "...idolatry so incenses and kindles the wrath of God, that it is never quenched till the offenders, and all they possess, be destroyed from the earth."[13] Knox made this radical argument on the basis of Deuteronomy 13. The following passage is worth noting, for Knox uses it as one of the most important grounds of his resistance theory:

> If your very own brother, or your son or daughter, or the wife you love, or your closest friend secretly entices you, saying, "Let us go and worship other gods" ...show him no pity. Do not spare him or shield him. You must certainly put him to death. Your hand must be the first in putting him to death, and then the hands of all the people. Stone him to death....[14]

Knox noted that Mosaic Law commanded that not only an individual but the community also was subject to the same punishment: if one of the

Israelite towns were led to an idolatry, the other Israelites had to destroy "all" who lived in it.[15]

Apparently, what Knox wanted to say by drawing on these passages was that even the private citizens may slay the Catholic sovereign Mary and her Catholic supporters. As we will see later, he actually advances to such a full-blown doctrine of active resistance in his 1558 writings. In the middle of the 1550s, however, he does not go so far. In the *Godly Letter* he restrains himself from legitimizing armed resistance to the ruler by the private citizens. To the hypothetical question of the reader of his *Letter*, "What then? Shall we go and slay all idolaters?", he recoils from the straight application of the above passages: "That were the office, dear brethren, of every civil magistrate....But of you is required only to avoid participation and company of their abominations, as well in body as in soul."[16]

To supplement his somewhat inconsistent position, Knox appeals to the episodes of king David and the apostle Paul in the Scriptures. Neither David in exile among the Philistines nor Paul surrounded by the idolaters in Corinth intended to slay anyone for the reason that he/she was an idolater. "Wherefore it is plain," says Knox, "that the slaying of idolaters appertains not to every particular man." The English Protestants had only to follow the course which David and Paul took: "I will not offer their drink offerings of blood, neither will I take their name in my mouth" (Ps. 16:4); "You may not be partakers of the Lord's table and of the table of the devils" (I Cor. 10:21). Knox will be content, at least at the moment, if his Protestant congregations "so abhor idolatry, that no part of the body be defiled therewith."[17]

Knox had a very high esteem of the prophetic office of the ministry. When the Catholics charged that he was inciting treason in advising the people not to obey the command of the queen to attend the Mass, he responded by appealing to the precedent of Jeremiah who exhorted the Jews to go and surrender to the foreign invader, king Nebuchadnezzar (Jeremiah 37). He said, "the prophet of God sometimes may teach treason against kings, and yet neither he, nor such as obey the word spoken in the Lord's name by him, offends God."[18] Knox was identifying himself as a contemporary prophet, saying, "I, a man sent of God...to call...this people...again to the true service of God...."[19] Doubtlessly, his prophetic self-consciousness was the source of his bold defiance against the tyrannical powers.

Ridley maintains that during the spring and summer of 1554, Knox developed the theory that the subjects of a Catholic sovereign could lawfully overthrow their sovereign by armed revolution.[20] Greaves even argues that Knox, in 1553-54, apparently called for open resistance against an idolatrous monarch.[21] As we have seen so far, however, these are misleading at least with regard to Knox's theory of armed resistance by the private citizens. Although he warned of the divine vengeance against the idolaters, until 1554 Knox was expressly prohibiting the private citizens from taking up arms. In *A Comfortable Epistle sent to the Afflicted Church of Christ, exhorting them to bear his Cross with Patience*, which was written in May, 1554, he again dissuaded the English Protestants from resorting to any violent action against the Queen and her Catholic supporters.[22] This position is maintained also in *A Faithful Admonition unto the Professors of God's Truth in England* which is believed to have been written in the Spring and the Summer of 1554. In this epistle, Knox attributes the designation of the instrument for the punishment of the idolaters exclusively to God: The means by which God shall perform his vengeance, says Knox, "neither appertains to thee to demand, nor to me to define."[23] Although he was ready to accept any means God should offer, he never overtly approved active resistance by the private citizens. In view of these evidences, it would be fair to conclude that during the first half of the 1550s, Knox was still adhering to the doctrine of passive disobedience, and that some apparently radical statements appearing in his *Godly Letter* were no more than incidental ones.

By this time, fear was increasingly growing about the future of all Protestantism. This concern was the result of the new policy adopted by the leading Catholic powers of Northern Europe. After years of vacillation and compromise, the Catholic princes had decided to reimpose religious unity by force.[24] At this time, Knox made a trip to Switzerland and met the most eminent Protestant leaders such as Calvin, Bullinger and Viret. In his interview with them, he asked four questions that were important to his political struggles: 1) whether the son of a king who is too young to rule is still to be regarded as a lawful sovereign; 2) whether a female can lawfully rule a kingdom and transfer the right of sovereignty to her husband; 3) whether obedience is to be rendered to a magistrate who enforces idolatry and condemns true religion; and whether the lesser magistrates in possession of military power can lawfully repel that ungodly violence; and 4) when the nobility resists an idolatrous sovereign by force, which party must the godly stand for?[25]

Calvin answered the critical third question with his usual conservative tone. "Under no circumstances," he said, is it justifiable for subjects to resist a ruler by force.[26] Bullinger's answers were more encouraging than Calvin's. He answered in part that "we must not obey the king or magistrate when their commands are opposed to God and his lawful worship." Bullinger went on: "...the Holy Scripture not only permits, but even enjoins upon the magistrate a just and necessary defense."[27]

Was Knox encouraged or discouraged after the trip to Switzerland? This is a question that is difficult to answer. The traditional view represented by J. H. Burns is that the answers of Calvin and Bullinger cooled Knox's ardor. Ridley and Greaves, on the contrary, feel that Bullinger's answers were sufficient to strengthen Knox's resolution.[28] Perhaps the best answer to this question will be given by comparing the *Godly Letter* with *A Faithful Admonition*, which were written respectively before and after his interview with the Swiss reformers. A comparison of the two documents shows that there is no significant difference between them with regard to his resistance theory. Since the answers of Calvin and Bullinger conflicted with each other to a considerable extent, it seems to have been difficult for Knox to take either position.

During the years prior to Knox's conversion to radicalism, events had been pushing him into a situation in which he could not but develop a theory of active resistance. Religious persecution was continuing to occur in England. In Scotland, Mary Stuart was about to marry a Frenchman, which meant an influx of French troops and the possibility of active persecution.[29] Furthermore, two impending events seem to have worked as a trigger for Knox's writing of his most radical 1558 tracts.

One event was the persecution against Knox by ecclesiastical authority. In the fall of 1555, Knox returned to Scotland and preached in different parts of the country for about one year. At the same time he administered the sacrament of the Lord's Supper in private houses to which many persons of distinction resorted. The signal success that attended Knox's ministry alarmed the prelates and instigated them to adopt measures to check his progress. Knox was summoned to appear before their Convocation in the Church of the Black Friars in Edinburgh in May 1556. But that diet was canceled for an unknown reason. No sooner had Knox returned to Geneva than the same proceedings were renewed. Naturally, Knox failed to appear before the Provincial Council. He was condemned as contumacious, declared a heretic, degraded from his priest's order, excommunicated, and sentenced to death. His effigy was burned at the Cross of Edinburgh.

The other incident concerned the nobility of Scotland. In May 1557, he received a letter from Scottish nobility, the content of which was that since the situation had become favorable to Protestants, he should return to Scotland. In response to the letter, Knox left Geneva and arrived at Dieppe in October. While waiting for the first ship to Scotland, he received the second letter from them. Its content was that they had reconsidered the invitation and that he should wait in Dieppe for their final decision. The true reason the nobility changed their minds was that in the critical stage of their negotiation with Mary the regent of Scotland on the marriage of her daughter Mary Queen of Scotland, to the Dauphin, they did not want to impair a successful bargain by the presence and preaching of Knox. A suspicion now emerged in Knox's mind regarding the nobilities' true motive and reliability for the establishment of Protestantism in Scotland. He came to think that they might be using the Protestant movement for a purely selfish and political end. He decided, therefore, to directly challenge them to do their duty for the Reformation in Scotland.[30]

Knox began his *Appellation Addressed to the Nobility and Estates of Scotland* by presenting the reason for which he asked them to protect him from the popish clergy. According to him, the nobles were powers ordained of God. Since God has appointed them "princes, with their kings," they had to "defend the innocent" who were oppressed.[31] Therefore, following the examples of Jeremiah and the apostle Paul, it was lawful for "the servants of God" to call for the help of the civil magistrate against juridical injustice done to them. Besides, he argued, the magistrates had the power to repress the clerical tyranny and absolve people from their condemnation.[32]

According to Knox, the purpose for which God has placed the magistrates over their brethren is twofold: the promotion of God's glory and the welfare of the people. The first goal could be achieved by maintaining the "true religion," and the second, by punishing malefactors and defending the innocent. It was not enough for the magistrates "to abstain from violent wrong and oppression." They were bound to rule for the spiritual and physical weal of their subjects. For their spiritual welfare, the magistrates had to provide "true pastors" on the one hand, and also repress the "tyranny of the bishops," punishing them "as thieves and murders, as idolaters and blasphemers."[33]

God would not accept the excuse of the magistrates, says Knox, that they had supposed religious matters to have been committed to their bishops. God would regard their permission of those unworthy bishops as "a participation with their theft and murder." Therefore, Knox declared, "the reformation of religion appertains to the civil magistrates and nobility."[34]

Knox goes on to deal with the issue of resistance to the secular power, especially to the regal authority. What are the lesser magistrates supposed to do under the tyranny of the king? After raising this question, Knox answers: by their "gravities, counsel, and admonition," the magistrates are "bound to correct and repress" whatever is expressly repugnant to God's Word. In Knox's view, it was a blasphemy to say, "We must obey our kings, be they good or be they bad; for God has so commanded," for it was tantamount to thinking of God as "an author and maintainer of all iniquity." Knox was rejecting conventional political thought when he said that those who obey the unjust commandment of the tyrant would bring in the divine punishment. They will be rewarded if they resist actively the unjust powers, and will be damned if they fail to do so.[35] When the tyrants violate God's glory or oppress the innocent people, believers do not have to obey. Rather, says Knox, God has "approved... and greatly rewarded" those who have disobeyed tyrants.[36]

It was in his *Appellation* that Knox made a full application of God's commands in Deuteronomy 13. He restrained himself from openly expressing his view four years before, when he was writing *Admonition to England*. He now sets forth two revolutionary points on the basis of this passage. The first point is that whoever provokes the people to idolatry ought to be put to death regardless of his/her social status. Even kings ought to be executed if they are proved to be idolaters. Secondly, the execution of the idolaters can be carried out not only by the chief magistrate, but also by "the whole body of that people," and "every member of the same, according to the vocation of every man, and to that possibility and occasion which God does administer...."[37] Knox was arriving at the revolutionary conclusion that even private citizens could lawfully resist the tyrants with violence. As Waltzer indicates, tyrannicide was "no longer the special mission of an inspired man; it had become the ordinary vocation of any man who would assume it."[38] This, indeed, was the first sanction of popular revolution by a Calvinist.

For Knox, to punish the idolatrous tyrant was not so much a right as a duty. It was the duty incurred by the covenant which exists between God and his people. Once a people has received "the true religion," each individual citizen was taken to have promised God to uphold all his laws. "...after the verity has been received and approved, ...not only the magistrates...but also the people are bound by that oath which they have made to God, to revenge to the uttermost of their power the injury done against his majesty."[39]

What if the people refuse to remove the iniquity from among them and continue to serve the tyrant? They would provoke the wrath of God against themselves, warned Knox, for they would be considered as involved in the "conspiracy against God." The notion that collective responsibility is created because of the iniquity committed by the ruler is characteristic of Knox:

> God will neither excuse nobility nor people... that obey and follow their kings in manifest iniquity; but with the same vengeance will God punish the prince, people, and nobility, conspiring together against him and his holy ordinances; as in the punishment taken upon Pharaoh, Israel, Juda and Babylon is evident to be seen.[40]

Having completed *The Appellation to the nobility*, Knox still could not be at rest, for he felt that "the nobles were changeable, unreliable and mercenary, and just as apt as pope or king to absorb for themselves what belonged to God."[41] Therefore, he set out to write another letter to the common people of Scotland. The result was *A Letter Addressed to the Commonalty of Scotland*. In this letter some of the themes reappear which were addressed to the nobility in the *Appellation*. It opens with an emphasis on the people's collective responsibility for the establishment and maintenance of true religion: they should not assume that the reformation and care of religion does not appertain to them because they are "no kings, judges, nobles, nor authority." On the contrary, they should make sure that their faith is grounded on the true Word of God.[42]

In spite of his admission that there was a social and civil distinction between the nobility and the people, Knox nevertheless asserted that in matters of religion, all individuals were equal. To drive his point home, Knox cited Moses' law concerning the tabernacle: God commanded every Israelite man to pay yearly a half sheckel for the maintenance of the tabernacle. The rich were not supposed to pay more, nor the poor less. "If this equality was commanded by God for the maintenance of that transitory tabernacle, which was but a shadow of a better one to come," declares Knox, "is not the same required of us who now have the verity, which is Jesus Christ?" To take the responsibility of maintaining the "true tabernacle," they had to demand that their superiors provide for them "true preachers" and expel the false ones, the Catholic priests. If the rulers refuse to do so,

> ...most justly you may provide true preachers for yourselves...them you may maintain and defend against all that shall persecute them...You may, moreover, withhold the fruits and profits which your false bishops and clergy most unjustly receive of you....[43]

For Knox, the religious issue was developing into a civil and political one of refusing to pay taxes.

Knox goes on to show that not to be involved actively in evil does not necessarily warrant one's innocence in the presence of God. As much as the Scottish common people were able, they had to carry out their duty by declaring themselves opposed to the Roman Catholicism. To keep silent was just another way of expressing their approval.

> And if you think that you are innocent, because you are not the chief authors of such iniquity, you are utterly deceived. For God does not only punish the chief offenders, but with them does he damn the consenters to iniquity; and all are judged to consent, that, knowing impiety committed, give no testimony that the same displeases them.[44]

In addition to the open disapproval of the rulers' iniquities the commonalty had also to take actions to get rid of them. Knox's belief was, as he pronounced later in the debate with Lethington, that God demanded one to oppose himself to "all iniquity, so far as into him lies."[45]

In the course of his search for a godly instrument for the reformation of religion in Scotland, Knox was contributing to the development of a democratic idea, namely, check and balance. His doctrine of checking the king by the nobility, and the nobility by the people, must have resulted in the distribution of power and the expansion of the opportunity for people's political participation.

The First Blast of the Trumpet against the Monstrous Regiment of Women, written toward the end of 1557, is primarily concerned with the issue of legitimacy of female government. Although most widely-known, it does not directly deal with the issue of resistance to the unjust power. In the summary of *Second Blast* (1558), however, Knox presents a very radical doctrine of the right of resistance to tyrants. The work sets forth four straightforward propositions: first, the legitimacy of the sovereign ruler is created not only by "propinquity of blood," but also by the ordinance of God which is confirmed through election. Second, a public office is not to be given to any manifest idolater or notorious transgressor of God's precepts. Third, it is lawful to disobey and remove the tyrant even after the oath and promise was made by the people. Fourth, if, either by rashness or by ignorance of the people, anyone unworthy of the chief magistrate is chosen as the ruler, it is most just for the people to depose and punish that person afterward.[46] The most significant aspect of *Second Blast* was that Knox provided for a more comprehensive recognition of the right of resistance. He was not talking primarily about the religious tyrants. All the tyrants, whether religious or political, were to be resisted and removed by the people.

A memorable occasion when Knox pronounced the lawfulness of revolution was his interview with Mary Stewart in 1561. When the interview came to the issue of obedience to the political power, Mary pointed out that he taught the people to receive a different religion than she could allow. She sharply asked, "How can that doctrine be of God, seeing that God commands subjects to obey their princes?" To this, Knox replied bluntly. Subjects had no obligation to "frame their religion" according to "the appetites of their princes," for the princes were often "the most ignorant of all others in God's true religion." After a while, Mary asked whether subjects might lawfully resist their princes with force. Knox responded: "If their princes exceed their bounds, and do against that wherefore they should be obeyed, it is no doubt but they may be resisted, even by power." Here he was presupposing the existence of the covenant between God and the princes.

Knox, using an illustration similar to one Calvin used in his *Institutes*, drew a conclusion exactly opposite to that of Calvin: If a father, stricken with a frenzy, attempts to slay his own children, then, the children may "join themselves together, apprehend the father, take the sword or other weapon from him, and finally bind his hands and keep him in prison, till his frenzy would be over past." Likewise, argued Knox, if the king, "in a very mad frenzy," attempts to murder the "children of God," it agreed with God's will for them to do the same as did the children in the above illustration. This would not be disobedience against princes, but rather "just obedience."[47]

In April 1563, some Catholic leaders celebrated the Mass in violation of the law. The Protestants were offended, but the Queen did nothing to punish them. Some of the Protestant leaders took action of their own accord and apprehended the violators. Mary summoned Knox and asked him to intervene for the arrested Catholics. Finding Knox's response to be cold, she pointed out that the punishment of the malefactors was under an exclusive jurisdiction of the prince. "Will you allow," asked Mary, "that they shall take my sword in their hands?" Knox replied that if a prince did not make proper use of the "sword of justice" God entrusted to them, others than the princes might punish the vice that is repugnant to God. This time, Knox called attention to the mutual covenant between the sovereign and subjects:

> Consider what it is that you ought to do unto them by mutual contract. They are bound to obey you, and that not but in God. You are bound to keep laws unto them. You crave of them service; they crave of you protection and defence against wicked doers. Now, Madam, if you shall deny your duty unto them...think you to receive full obedience of them? I fear, Madam. You shall not.[48]

At the General Assembly in 1564, a dispute took place between Knox and Maitland of Lethington. When it came to the question of the subject's duty to obey or resist a wicked prince, Knox restated the views. he had been enunciating since 1558: subjects were bound not only to obey the powers, but to resist them actively when their commands were contrary to God's commands.

In this debate Knox introduced a vital distinction between the person and the ordinance. Interpreting the key-word "powers" in Romans 13:1-2, he insisted that power given unto a human being was one thing, and the person clad with the power was another. This distinction, in turn, was based on his observation of Rom.13:3-4 regarding the purpose of divine ordination and of the propensity of human rulers. While "God's ordinance is the conservation of mankind, the punishment of vice, the maintaining of virtue," the persons of power are "commonly profane, unjust....and subject to corruption...."[49]

Accordingly, although the subjects were forbidden to resist the authority itself, they could lawfully resist the individuals placed in that position. This separation of the ordinance and the person led Knox to employ the private-law theory, according to which, if the king committed a flagrant crime, he was not to be treated as a king but as an ordinary offender. As Knox states:

> ...kings have no privilege more than has the people to offend God's majesty; and if... so they do, they are no more exempted from the punishment of the law than any other subject....if the king be one murderer, adulterer, or idolater, he should suffer according to God's law, not as one king, but as one offender, and the people may put God's laws in execution....[50]

The most insightful point made by Knox in this dispute was his interpretation of the background of Calvin's passive position held by Maitland. When Maitland, appealing to Calvin, insisted that none but God could punish a tyrant, Knox responded by arguing that the limit of Christian resistance to the tyrants was to be determined by the realistic evaluation of their power in a particular socio-political situation. In Knox's judgment, Calvin

> spoke of Christian subjects under the tyrants and infidels, so dispersed that they have no other force but only to sob to God for deliverance.... But my argument has another ground; for I speak of the people assembled together in one body of any commonwealth, unto whom God has given sufficient force, not only to resist, but also to suppress all kind of open idolatry....[51]

Knox's God was a realist. He did not impose upon all Christians the same amount of political responsibility. To this also was applied the axiom: "From everyone who has been given much, much will be demanded; and from the one who has been entrusted with much, much more will be asked" (Luke 12:48). As Kyle observes regarding Knox's view on this subject:

> Though he acknowledged the pre-Constantinian church as an acceptable model when believers were but a minority, he insisted that Christians in sufficient numbers must establish a Christian commonwealth modeled on the Old Testament.[52]

Relationship between Church and State

At first glance Knox appears to hold a contradictory view of the relationship between church and state. Sometimes, he seems to be an Erastian, while at other times, he gives evidence of being a theocrat. On the one hand, he claimed that the chief goal of the government was to glorify God and protect the true religion. On the other hand, he believed that no power on earth was above the civil authority. He even insisted on the jurisdiction of the state over the church.[53] This apparent contradiction is resolved, however, when we understand "theocracy" as God's rule as distinguished from "ecclesiocracy," the rule of the church.

Knox elevated the office of civil authority primarily because he wanted to destroy papal absolutism. As Gray states, Knox used the idea of kingly supremacy "to kill papal supremacy." When he found, however, that kings had the same tendency to usurp God's place, he proceeded to attack the regal supremacy by bringing in the nobility. As the nobility revealed the similar inclination, he turned to the common people, in whom he found the real strength for the Scottish religious reformation.

> He thus used the king against the pope, the nobles against the king, the subjects against king and nobles, and the church against all. His one travail was that all should obey God. Apart from that, he did not greatly care who obeyed whom. The means whereby he procured obedience to the divine command were largely a matter of chance and circumstance. He was willing to become an Erastian or anti- Erastian to advocate at one time the divine right of kings and at another the divine right of rebellion, and that without conscious hypocrisy or real inconsistency.[54]

For Knox, church and state were separate institutions. Each was directly responsible to God. Knox wanted the role of the state to be limited with regard to the church: 1) to support the true religion and suppress idolatry; 2) to act as a higher court of judicature from a corrupt church, as he insisted in *The Appellation to the Nobility*. In this case, however, there had to be the provision that the members who were appealing could reject the state's decisions if they were contrary to Scripture; 3) to take the responsibility of supporting the church in terms of finance; 4) to punish vices repugnant to God as well as crimes; and 5) to remove the ungodly magistrates.[55]

Knox believed also that the church should neither dictate to the magistrates nor control the state, as the Scottish Catholic church had done. He objected to the employment of pastors in the civil government. He was by no means an ecclesiocrat:

> Let none that be appointed to labor in Christ's vineyard be entangled with civil affairs...If once God's true religion were established, there would be eno need forthe ministers to come to parliament.[56]

This does not mean, however, that Knox prohibited the ministers from addressing contemporary political issues in the pulpit. Rather, he stressed and practiced the right of the ministers to deal with the political questions from a prophetic perspective. "He would tolerate no restrictions when it came to preaching God's Word, and the Word of God recognized no distinctions between religious and civil affairs. He believed that a man of God must speak as directed by the Holy Spirit, regardless of the subject matter."[57] When Knox preached against Queen Mary's marriage to a Catholic prince, Mary was infuriated and summoned him. She complained to Knox about his meddling in civil affairs. He denied the charge, however, except when in "the preaching place," adding: "there, Madam, I am not master of myself, but must obey him who commands me to speak plain, and to flatter no flesh upon the face of the earth."[58]

Knox's Political Influence

All these writings and efforts of Knox were not in vain. In December 1557 the Scottish nobility came to sign a solemn league and covenant by which they constituted themselves "the Congregation of Christ" binding themselves to resist their Catholic opponents, "the Congregation of Satan." Thus Knox provided Scotland with the ideological basis for "the first successful Calvinist Revolution."[59]

Knox exercised an enormous influence on the development of Calvinist political ideas. What prevailed among Calvinists after 1560 was Knox's view rather than Calvin's.[60] The seventeenth century Puritans readily accepted Knox's covenant idea and expressed it in both the Westminster Confession of Faith and the Westminster *Larger Catechism*. The second *Book of Discipline*, which set forth the covenant idea very clearly, became the basis for resistance to James VI/I and Charles I. Samuel Rutherford who accepted Knox's covenant idea presented it in his work *Lex Rex*, which, according to Reid, exerted a great impact on Scottish thinking and "was basic to the whole covenant movement during the latter part of the seventeenth century."[61]

THEODORE BEZA AND HIS RESISTANCE THEORY

The reader of *The Rights of Magistrates* written by Theodore Beza in 1574 is surprised to find that Calvin's successor could be so radical in his political ideas. Although less than ten years had passed since the death of Calvin, Beza's political ideas had developed so much from his predecessor's that if Calvin had had an opportunity to read his successor's work, he could not but have been shocked by it. As we will see later, such a drastic difference was caused by the different political situations in which they lived.

As early as 1554, Theodore Beza, or de Beze (1519-1605), already enunciated his doctrine of resistance to the tyrants by the inferior magistrates in his *De Haereticis a civili Magistratu Puniendis*:

> When then several princes abuse their office, whoever still feels it necessary to refuse to use the Christian magistrates offered by God against external violence whether of the unfaithful or of heretics, I charge, deprives the Church of God of a most useful, and... necessary defence.[62]

There seems some exaggeration in Kingdon's reference to the above passage as "one of the first justifications of popular right to overthrow tyrannical government ever expressed by a Calvinist," for Beza acknowledged here just the lesser magistrates' right to resist tyrants. As we will see later, Beza denied the private citizens' right of active resistance. It is likely, however, that it was at least one of the first explicit justifications of active resistance to the tyrant by the lesser magistrates.[63]

It was his experience of the Massacre of St. Bartholomew's Day in 1572 that led Beza to elaborate his theory of resistance to a surprisingly radical extent in *The Right of Magistrates over their Subjects.* This small book was the answer to the long-standing question of the many thousand Huguenots who had experienced the nightmare of the Massacre: "Is it for each to seize the sword and sally forth? Or does duty demand this tyranny to be suffered without resistance?"[64]

Beza begins his treatise with the question, "Must magistrates always be obeyed as unconditionally as God?" Beza's answer was that disobedience to the magistrates was to be reserved for two cases: when their commands were either "irreligious" or "iniquitous." By "irreligious" commands, he meant those which "order us to do what the First Table of God's Law forbid," or "forbid us to do what it commands." By "iniquitous," he meant that which "cannot be obeyed without violating or neglecting the charity we owe our fellow men according to our station." This indicated significant progress in Calvinist resistance theory, for Calvin permitted the right of disobedience only when the issue was directly concerned with the religion.[65]

Beza classifies the tyrants into two kinds: one is the kind of usurper who "in violation of law laid down and received usurps tyranny over their fellow citizens," and the other is the kind who "not content with that absolute power which they rightly acquire over their own people, extend their dominions at the cost of their neighbor's liberty...."[66] In Beza's view, the former was entirely different from the latter since people were "by no obligation bound" and "in no way subject" to the usurper.[67]

When a tyrant belongs to the first category, the responsibility of resistance falls upon the magistrates first.

> Where someone would seize dominion without title or has already usurped it...the private citizen should appeal to the legitimate magistrates so that, if possible, the public enemy may be repulsed by public authority and by common consent.[68]

A notable aspect in this remark is the indication that even after the usurpation was successfully carried out, the usurper had to be abolished. This provides an interesting contrast with Calvin's position. In his *Institutes*, Calvin insisted that legitimacy should be acknowledged to whomever presently holds power without respect to the process through which someone has come to it.[69] Beza was far more interested than his predecessor in the matter of legitimacy of power.

The second group responsible for the protection of the legitimacy of the government was, according to Beza, the private citizens: "if the magistrates, from connivance or whatever, should fail to do their duty [against the usurpation]," declares Beza, "then the private citizen should exert all his strength to defend the legitimate institutions of his country...and to resist an individual whose authority is not legitimate...."[70] This is another point of difference between Beza and Calvin. While Calvin argued that only a divinely inspired man was entitled to revolt against a tyrant, Beza repudiated such a notion. As far as the usurper-tyrant was concerned, anybody could take forcible action against him:

> ...however it may be true that those judges of the people of Israel were moved and stirred to the performance of those famous deeds by some divine and exceptional instinct, yet it does not immediately follow that Israelites themselves, whether holding office or even as private citizens, could not in accordance with their ordinary right have expelled the tyranny of strangers who had been neither elected nor approved by the people.[71]

"Why is it then," Beza imagines someone asking, "that in the Book of Judges, all the revolts are performed by the person who had an extraordinary divine calling?" Beza replies: The Book of Judges was not describing the norm but the facts, the facts as a divine scourge to the people's sin. In other words, if the Israelites had been in a right relationship with God, the individual Israelite could have demonstrated his/her sound spiritual conditions by tyrannicide:

> But that those liberations were effected by means of those men alone whom God summoned forth in a special way, does not go to dispose my contention, but rather demonstrates that the spirit of Israelites had for their transgression stunned and broken by the just judgment of God.[72]

Although the usurpers had to be punished even by the private citizens, they were not hopeless. In this respect, Beza shows himself to be as much of a realist as his predecessor. There was hope even for the usurpers. Even if they began as illegitimate rulers, they could still change themselves into legitimate ones. The prescription was to obtain the "free and lawful consent" of the people. This was another difference between Beza's political outlook and Calvin's. In Calvin, the sole source of legitimacy of the regime was the ordination of God. Beza, however, adds one more element for the legitimacy of power, the people's will and election.

> ...defect [of title] at the beginning of a usurpation may subsequently be repaired. He who began as a tyrant may become a legitim ate and inviolable magistrate through that free and lawful consent by which legitimate rulers are created.[73]

Although popular consent constituted legitimacy of power, there still could be a case for that consent being regarded as inadequate. When it was in conflict with the principle of "equity and honesty," the human will was invalid:

> ...the consent of the people or its greater part, whether given freely or extorted through fear and violence, should not be kept, but broken, if it appears to be in manifest conflict with equity and honesty.[74]

If the remedy for the usurper was relatively simple, the case of a legitimate sovereign who has degenerated into a tyrant was a much more complicated one. The remedy for this case depended on who the subject was. Beza classified all the subjects into three kinds: private persons, lesser magistrates, and the estates.

Private citizens did not have a right to resist a legitimate ruler, even if he/she was a notorious tyrant. The private citizen, for Beza, was not still a complete political agent: "unless a private person has a special calling from God, he may not, on his own initiative, answer force with force." For private citizens, passive disobedience was the maximum allowable: "it behooves him either to depart from the realm...and change his domicile or bear the yoke of the tyrant patiently by taking refuge with God in prayer."[75] The prescription of Beza for private persons confronting the unjust authority was not much different from Calvin's.

One reason why private citizens ought not resist the legitimate ruler was because they were regarded as having made a covenant with the ruler:

> ...a ruler who has been approved and accepted by his people, though he abuse his power, yet retains the basis of his authority as against his own private subjects, since an obligation entered upon publicly and by mutual consent cannot be dissolved and broken by the will of any private citizen.[76]

Once people think lightly of the contract with the ruler, Beza feared, the society will be swallowed up by the "endless disorders." In Beza's view, anarchy was "worse than the tyranny itself." He could not bear to see that "in the place of a single tyrant...a thousand would" come into power.[77]

Another reason Beza forbade private citizens to resist the legitimate ruler was Scriptural. Beza understood that St. Paul's and St. Peter's injunction to obey the powers was given for private citizens, if not for all the subjects. The apostles gave such a command in spite of their knowledge as to "what nature the Caesars then were." Moreover, the martyrs set an example for us by following the apostles' instruction while being persecuted by the most inhuman tyrants.[78]

The second kind of subjects were the lesser magistrates, who held a lower rank between the sovereign and the people. In order to justify resistance to the tyrants by lesser magistrates, Beza distinguished the sovereign from the sovereignty. The lesser magistrates were dependent not upon the person of the sovereign magistrate but upon the sovereign magistracy as such.

> ...although all these officers are beneath their sovereign in that they take commands from him and are installed in office and approved by him, they hold, properly speaking, not of the sovereign but of the sovereignty. That is why, when the sovereign magistrate dies, they nevertheless remain in office, just as the sovereignty itself remains intact.[79]

Beza saw the relationship between the supreme and the lesser magistrate as a contractual one. Therefore, the obligation that existed between those two parties was mutual. It meant that if the king clearly departed from "the conditions under which he was recognized and approved as king," it went without saying that

> the lesser magistrates of the kingdom, of the cities, and of the provinces...are free of their oath, at least to the extent that they are entitled to resis agrat oppression of the realm which they swore to defend and protect according to their office and their particular jurisdiction.[80]

When they were "reduced to such unavoidable compulsion," to offer resistance to the tyranny and "safeguard those within their care" was not at all seditious or disloyal action, but rather "loyal" and faithful action toward those who appointed them in their offices.[81]

The third class of subjects, according to Beza, was the Estates and similar bodies. With regard to resistance to the monarchy, these had the greatest authority. True, these were subject to the sovereign "in a certain respect." In other respects, however, the estates were the protector of the rights of "the sovereignty itself." For that purpose, it was sometimes expected for them "to hold the sovereign to his duty, and even, if needs be, to constrain and punish him."[82]

What was to be done if the Estates did not take any action against tyranny? Such incidents could happen because of intimidation or bribery by the tyrant. In such a case, private persons still did not have any remedy but "penitence and patience joined with prayers." But they could go to the lesser magistrates and ask them to do their duty, that is, to "join together and press for a convocation of the Estates."[83]

Throughout this treatise Beza upheld his theory of resistance with three basic assumptions: popular sovereignty, the social contract, and the reign of the law.

First, Beza had at least the embryo of the idea of popular sovereignty. He believed that all power, however supreme or great, "derives from the power of the public that put them in their station." It was evident to him that in the beginning, people did not originate from rulers, but the rulers were created for the sake of the people.

Was this idea of popular sovereignty not in conflict with the idea that all powers are ordained of God? Beza's answer to that was negative. God effected his ordination through the human channel, that was, election. King David was cited as an example:

> Although God expressly designated David, he still had to be elected by the people, who dutifully obeyed the will of God in choosing him.... and although the crown, by God's ordinance, was hereditary in the house of David, the

people, as long as they were free, chose as they pleased among the children of a deceased king....[84]

Second, Beza's resistance theory was based on the idea of contract, or covenant. Like John Knox, he derived this covenant idea from the Old Testament. When he read the history of Joash, the king of Judah, he found two covenants: 1) the oath by which a king and his people obligated themselves to God by promising to uphold His Law, and 2) a mutual oath between the king and the people. Beza concentrated on the second kind of covenant. When he observed the history of the nations, he found that wherever "law and equity" prevailed, nations never accepted kings "except upon definite conditions." There was never a nation "so unmindful" of its interests as to submit itself to the sovereign without attaching the "condition, expressed or implied," that he/she must govern "justly and equitably."[85]

For Beza, the existence of the contract implied that when there was a manifest violation of its "essential condition in consideration of which the obligation was contracted," the contract was dissolved and the obligation nullified. According to the law of nature and equity, the people who had the power to give rulers authority also had the power to deprive them of it.[86]

Third, Beza put a strong emphasis on the rule of law. The supreme ruler was not above the law, but the law was above the king. The insistence that the king was not subject to the law was nothing but a deceitful maxim of detestable flatterers. Though the ruler made the laws, he/she had to obey them.

Beza did not argue, however, that the king was to be bound by all laws indiscriminately. To the civil laws the ruler was not bound so much as the private citizens were. To the public laws and the so-called constitutional law, however, the ruler was no less bound than the private citizens were. Needless to say, the ruler was subject to divine or natural law.

Noteworthy in Beza's treatise are his answers to objections to his arguments. Interestingly, these answers are virtually the reversal of most essential points that Calvin made to defend his theory of non-resistance.

When some insisted that the tyrants were to be obeyed since they were divine punishments for the collective sin of the people, Beza responded by employing the private-law theory and just self-defense theory. To help explain his points, he used an illustration of a man who met robbers on the highway. It was true that no one was murdered without the consent of God. It was also true, however, that one had the legal right to resist the robbers. Such an action of resistance was regarded as a just self-defence unless God had given a special revelation for him to be slain by the robbers. It was, however, almost impossible to expect such a revelation. Therefore, Beza maintained,

> Legitimate self-defense against a tyrant, as against any criminal, is permissible unless God has expressly demanded the contrary. For although all things happen by God's will, His providence cannot be anticipated in a specific situation unless it has been expressly revealed. In the absence of such revelation, one must act according to God's general commands.[87]

To Beza, there seemed to be no evidence that tyrants were sent according to God's will. If someone argued that everything that existed was by God's will, then, Beza could argue that to succeed in eliminating the tyrants by active resistance was also possible by God's will. The fact that someone was, at the moment, in possession of the power proved nothing for Beza with respect to the legitimacy of his or her regime. Although many people, including Calvin, insisted that it was God who gave the kingdoms and empires to whomever he wanted to give them, and that, therefore, it was with the approval of God that someone succeeded in usurpation, Beza did not think so: "the favorable or adverse result alone," he argued, did not prove whether anything was just or unjust.[88]

Another common objection was regarding who had the right to punish the tyrant. The traditional attitude was that since the rulers were ordained by God, they were accountable only and immediately to God. Consequently, the supreme ruler had no other judge than God himself, "no matter how iniquitous or cruel they may be." King David was cited again as an example to support this view: though an adulterer and a wicked slayer of men, yet he was judged by no mortal men.

Beza was of a different opinion. As was previously noted, Beza thought that since the legitimacy of power was established not only by divine ordination but by the process of popular election, the ruler was responsible not only to God but also to the people. In other words, people had the right to punish the tyrant when he/she was in obvious conflict with God. The reason the Israelites did not punish the tyrant was, in Beza's view, because they "reserved" the right to do it. Furthermore, Beza asserted, King David could not be counted among the numbers of the ordinary tyrants. There was a great difference between him who had "on one occasion" fallen into sin and those who were "abandoned to every kind of crime."[89] Therefore, states Beza, if the sovereign departs from the good laws and conditions they have sworn to uphold and became notorious tyrants,

> ...it is the right of lesser magistrates to provide for themselves and those within their care by resisting flagrant tyranny. And the Estates of the country, or a similar body, to whom such authority is given by law, can and should resist according to his crime...[90]

Calvin used the patience of David with Saul as one of his most important grounds for obedience to the tyrants. But Beza did not agree with Calvin on this point. David's behavior in that case could not be taken as showing a general principle. It could not prove that all armed resistance was unlawful.

The case of Zedekiah should be taken in a similar way. He was punished not for his revolt against Nebuchadnezzar, but for his disobedience to Gods' specific and express command for him to surrender to the invader. Therefore, this case had nothing to do with the lawfulness or unlawfulness of active resistance to the tyrant.

That God commanded the Jews to pray for Nebuchadnezzar and the peace of Babylon did not imply that to pray for a tyrant was a general principle of God. It was a particular command for a particular generation of the Jews.

Someone insisted that as Jesus did not revolt, but paid tribute to Tiberius Caesar who was a usurper in Judea as well as a tyrant, we also should obey tyrants. In Beza's view, however, it was because Jesus did not come to this world to rule in human fashion. Rather, renouncing his prerogatives, he chose to live on earth as one of the private citizens. Besides, the Roman usurpation had been accepted by that time as an irrevocable reality by the more powerful majority of Jews: "We have no king but Caesar."[91]

Many people emphasized obedience to the tyrants on the grounds that the authorities ordained of God must be respected and that they were conducive to the maintenance of public order. Beza's view was exactly the opposite:

> ...neither can the authority of rulers be rendered secure nor can the public peace be maintained unless careful precautions be taken that tyranny may not steal in or if it has already stolen in that it be neither abolished or expelled.[92]

Still others maintained that the only remedy for the tyrant was prayer. Beza agreed that prayer was indispensable for the Christians in the face of the tyrant. Without prayer, said Beza, "any other remedy, no matter how lawful it may be, involves the danger of God's curse." However, this did not mean that prayer was the exclusive remedy. Even then, Beza admitted, there may be prayers or imprecations against the tyrant, like those Christians who prayed against Julian the Apostate.[93]

Some pointed out that the revolt of the Israelites against the tyrant Rehoboam was condemned. Beza explained that they were condemned not because they revolted against the tyrant, but because they did so "in an unlawful manner." Beza proposed three conditions for the rebellion to be lawful: 1) the tyranny has become thoroughly obvious, 2) no recourse to arms until all other remedies have been tried, 3) careful consideration of what is expedient, lest the cure be worse than the disease.[94]

Beza's Influence and Historical Significance

In the sixteenth century, the national sovereign states were emerging in Europe, threatening the rights and liberty of the people by the theories of centralization and absolutism. Although less than two decades had passed since the publication of the last version of the *Institutes,* the political situation had become far more acute. The need to exercise the right of resistance had become stronger. At this critical moment of history, Beza's *De jure Magistratuum* played a decisive role for the defence of the rights and liberty of the people. It provided the people with the Christian principles to which they could appeal under the tyrannical oppression and injustice.[95]

Schelven indicates that Beza's doctrines and expositions introduced in this small book are found in several famous documents: 1) the "Plakkaat van Verlating" of 1581 by which the Netherlands States-General renounced the allegiance of the Seventeen Netherlands to Philip of Spain; 2) the American Declaration of Independence; 3) the French Declaration of the Rights of Man and the Citizen, which agitated the Revolution of 1789; and even 4) the Atlantic Charter, which is the twentieth century edition of Beza's principles. If so, it would not be a mere exaggeration to say, as Schelven does, that "A new era was inaugurated by Calvin's successor after the St. Bartholomew's Night in the pages of his *De jure Magistratuum*."[96]

Conclusion

On the whole, considerable grounds seem to exist for the argument that there is an apparent difference between Calvin's political doctrines and those of his followers. The latter were far more radical than the former, especially in their resistance theory. While Calvin was very careful to issue a sanction to active resistance, Knox and Beza developed the possibility of resistance to the full. Knox even reached the justification of the popular revolution, not to mention tyrannicide.

It would be an exaggeration, however, to say that Calvin's resistance theory and that of Beza and Knox are completely different from each other. Rather, it is closer to the truth to say that the latter two were a continuation and development of the former. It should never be underestimated that by introducing the 'ephors' passage, Calvin opened the door to resistance to tyrants by the popular magistrates. Moreover, toward the end of his life, i. e., after 1560, Calvin increasingly tended to concede lawfulness of active resistance to unjust political powers. That is to say, the difference between Calvin's resistance theory and that of the Calvinists can best be seen as a matter of degree.

But this difference in degree is not a trivial one. Living in almost the same age, Calvin's general approach and attitude to political power was very cautious and conservative, whereas Knox and Beza showed no hesitancy to advocate active resistance to tyrants.

What brought about such a significant difference between the teacher and his disciples? In Knox's case, temperamental factors seem to have played a considerable role as the cause of his radicalism. In Allen's words, while Calvin was "coldly intellectual and severely self-restrained," Knox was "hot and violent and impatiently eager....honest and outspoken, even to boorishness." He did not have Calvin's juristic knowledge and training. He "never thought in terms of law." He resembled Luther or

Latimer rather than Calvin.[97] Regarding Beza, the temperament theory also appears to be applicable to some extent. Although he too studied law as a profession, his "natural urge lay in the direction of literature and poetry rather than in the definition and consideration of legal relations in human society."[98]

It would be unfair, however, to place too much stress on the temperamental aspect of Beza and Knox as the cause of their differences from their teacher in their resistance theory. The decisive reason is to be found, rather, in the difference of the situations in which they were located. Calvin could carry out his reformation successfully at least partly owing to the favor and support of his Genevan magistrates. For such a person, it would have been difficult to develop a radical theory of resistance to the political authority.

On the contrary, Knox and his fellow Protestants constantly confronted and were sometimes persecuted by these temporal powers who rigorously advocated Roman Catholicism. Mary Tudor of England and Mary Stuart of Scotland were but two symbols for the secular authority that opposed and oppressed Knox throughout his life. Beza did not have any serious opposing political powers in Geneva. His radicalism was caused by the incidents which had been occurring in France, his native country. After the Massacre of St. Bartholomew's Day, it must have been increasingly difficult for Beza to see the French Huguenots being persecuted by the tyranny of an absolute Catholic monarchy. Finally he reached the point where it became impossible for him to refrain from issuing a treatise which equipped his French Protestant brothers and sisters with the theological grounds for active resistance to tyrants. That was why he tenaciously attempted to publish his book at the risk of the safety of Geneva, in departure from his predecessor in one of the important topics in political theory.[99]

The most radical and significant element in Knox's doctrine of resistance was that even the private citizen was entitled to actively resist the idolatrous tyrant. For him, this was not so much a right as a duty for every Christian.

While Knox tended to address himself mainly to religious tyranny, Beza did not confine his discussion to religious matters. He insisted on the right of resistance to a tyrant regardless of the content of the tyranny. In this respect, he can be said to have been more comprehensive than Knox.

In terms of the agent of resistance, however, he was less inclusive than Knox, for he denied the right of active resistance by private citizens.

By combining the theories of Beza and Knox, we possess an almost complete theory of revolution, i.e., the right of every citizen to revolt against any kind of unjust power. It is no wonder that wherever Calvinism was disseminated, the established old order was challenged. Like the apostles, Calvinists were "trouble makers all over the world" (Act 17:6; 24:5) In the Scottish Revolution, the English Puritan Revolution, the Dutch struggle for independence from Spain, the French religious war, and the American Revolution, Calvinism contributed much to public commotions, the overturning of governments, and social and political experimentation.

1 Ronald VanderMolen, "Political Calvinism," *Journal of Church and State*, 11 (1969), 461-2.

2 J.W.Allen, *A History of Political Thought in the Sixteenth Century* (London, Methuen, 1951), 315, 107.

3 Richard L. Greaves, *Theology and Revolution in the Scottish Reformation: Studies in the Thought of John Knox* (Christian University Press, 1980), 126.

4 For a detailed discussion of Tyndale's doctrine of non- resistance, see Jasper Ridley, *John Knox* (Oxford University Press, 1968), 172-4, and, for English doctrine of non-resistance, refer to Allen, *A History*, 125-133.

5 John Knox, "Epistle to the Congregation of Berwick," quoted in Peter Lorimer, *John Knox and the Church of England* (London, 1875), 259.

6 John Knox, "A Confession and Declaration of Prayer," in David Laing, ed. *The Works of John Knox* (Edinburgh, 1895) 3: 83-107.

7 *Works*, 3:166.

8 For example, W. Stanford Reid states, "Basic to Knox's thought on political government was the concept of the covenant...." Reid, "John Knox's Theology of Political Government," Sixteenth Century Journal 19, No. 4 (1988), 529, 532; Greaves asserts that Knox's "concept of disobedience cannot be properly understood without a knowledge of covenant obligations and relationship." Greaves, *Theology and Revolution*, 136-7.

9 *Works* 3: 190-1.

10 *Ibid.*, 3:193.

11 Reid, 529.

12 *Works*. 3:193.

13 *Ibid.*, 3:193.

14 Deut. 13:6-11.

15 Deut. 13:12-16.

16 *Works*, 3:194.

17 *Ibid.*, 3:195.

18 *Works*, 3:184.

19 *Ibid.*, 4:474.

20 Ridley, 171.

21 Greaves, 134.

22 *Works*, 3:239-249.

23 *Ibid*., 3:325.

24 Quentin Skinner, *The Foundations of Modern Political Thought* (Cambridge University Press, 1978), 189.

25 *Works*, 4:221-25.

26 John Calvin, Letter to Bullinger, 29 Apr. 1554, in Julet Bonnet, *Letters of John Calvin*, 4 vols. (New York), 3; 37-8.

27 The whole content of Bullinger's answers to Knox's questions was enclosed in his letter to Calvin written on the 26th of March 1554. See, *Works*, 3:221-6.

28 J.H.Burns, "John Knox and Revolution," *History Today* 8 (Aug. 1958), 567-8; Ridley, 179-180; Greaves, 130-4.

29 Richard Kyle, *The Mind of John Knox* (Lawrence: Colorado Press, 1984), 266; Greaves, 138; Reid, 534.

30 Kyle, 261-2.

31 *Works*, 4:469, 497, 498.

32 *Ibid*., 4:469-476.

33 *Ibid*., 4:481-4.

34 *Ibid*., 4:484-5. To support his view, Knox indicates that in the Scripture, God did not exempt the matters of religion from the power of Moses, instead, that he committed them all to his care. Moreover, says Knox, God commanded Aaron to depend on Moses even in the religious matters. The fact that Moses called Aaron and accused him of the making of the golden calf was, for Knox, a sure evidence that the magistrates had the jurisdiction over the clergy. Knox also considered that the examples of the Old Testament kings such as Asa, Jehoshaphat, Hezekiah, and Josiah proved the power and duties of the civil magistrate in the reformation of religion (4:486-7, 509).

35 Skinner, 238. In order to be able to understand Knox's calling on the nobility for the armed resistance to the tyrants, we need to take the contemporary semi-feudal conditions into account: Scottish nobles could and did have private armies and the right of jurisdiction within their own areas. "The situation was fairly close to the conditions in Sparta as Calvin had described them, where the ephors shared control with the chief magistrates" (Gray, 137; Kyle, 292).

36 *Works*, 4: 495-6, 490.

37 *Ibid*., 4: 499-501, 503-4.

38 Michael Waltzer, *The Revolution of the Saints* (Harvard University Press, 1965), 108.

39 *Works*, 4:506.

40 *Ibid.*, 4:498, 507. Knox reiterates these ideas in his *Brief Exhortation to England* in 1559: When Mary sought to establish idolatry, she had to be executed. Negligence of this duty had made the English guilty of murdering their fellow humans, denying God, and committing treason to God (5:516-19).

41 John R. Gray, "The Political Theory of John Knox," *Church History* 8 (June, 1939), 139; Kyle, 293.

42 *Works*, 4:526-7.

43 *Ibid.*, 4:534.

44 *Ibid.*, 4: 535, 536-7.

45 *Ibid.*, 4:537; 2:440; Gray, 142.

46 *Ibid.*, 4:539-40.

47 *Ibid.*, 2:282.

48 *Ibid.*, 2:370-6.

49 *Ibid.*, 2:436.

50 *Ibid.*, 2:451-2. As an example of this, Knox suggests the case of Uzzias, the king of Juda in the Old Testament.

51 *Ibid.*, 2:442-443.

52 Kyle, 290.

53 *Works.*, 4:324.

54 *Gray*, 144-5.

55 *Reid*, 538; Kyle, 294.

56 *Works*, 5:519.

57 Gray, 144.

58 *Works.*, 2:387.

59 P. Hume Brown, *History of Scotland*, vol. 2: From the Accession of Mary Stuart to the Revolution of 1689 (Cambridge, 1902), 48, 57-73, cited in Skinner, *The Foundations*, 238.

60 Allen, 107.

61 Reid, 539.

62 Beza, *De Haereticis*, 133. quoted in Robert M. Kingdon, "The First Expression of Theodore Beza's Political Ideas," *Archiv fur Reformationsgeschichte* 46 (1955), 92.

63 It is true that Calvin also admitted in his *Institutes* that the popular magistrates can repress and bridle the tyrants' abuse of their power. However, the expression was not so overt and express as Beza's.

64 A.A.Schelven, "Beza's De Iure Magistratuum in Subditos," *Archiv fur Reformationsgeschichte* 45 (1954): 72.

65 Theodore Beza, *Concerning the Rights of Rulers over their Subjects and the Duty of Subjects toward Their Rulers*, trans., Henry Louis Gonin, ed., A.H.Murray (Cape Town, 1956), 25; For a better understanding of the original *De jure*, refer also to *Constitutionalism and Resistance in the Sixteenth Century: Three Treatises by Hotman, Beza, and Mornay*, trans. and ed., Julian H. Franklin, (New York, 1969), 101. From now on, the two translations will be juxtaposed in the footnotes.

66 Murray, 32.

67 Murray, 37.

68 Franklin, 106-7; Murray, 34.

69 See, Calvin, *Institutes*, IV, 20, 22-28.

70 Franklin, 107; Murray, 34.

71 Murray, 34.

72 Murray, 34.

73 Franklin, 107; Murray, 34.

74 Franklin, 107; Murray, 35.

75 Franklin, 108. Murray, 36-7.

76 Murray, 37; Franklin, 109.

77 Murray, 37.

78 Murray, 37-8; Franklin, 109.

79 Franklin, 111; Murray, 38-9.

80 Franklin, 111-2; Murray, 40.

81 Franklin, 112; Murray, 41.

82 Franklin, 113.

83 Franklin, 129-130; Murray, 72.

84 Franklin, 117-8; Murray, 51-2.

85 Franklin, 114, 124; Murray, 44-45, 64.

86 Franklin, 114, 124; Murray, 64, 45.

87 Franklin, 131; Murray, 77-8.

88 Murray, 33.

89 Murray, 68-9.

90 Franklin, 124; Murray, 63.
91 Franklin, 131; Murray, 79.
92 Murray, 29; Franklin, 103.
93 Franklin, 131; Murray, 78-9.
94 Franklin, 130-131.
95 Murray, Foreword, vi.
96 Schelven, "Beza's De Iure," 77-8.
97 Allen, 107; Gray, 134.
98 Shelven, 76.
99 Beza completed this book in 1573 and asked the Council of the city of Geneva to agree to its publication. The Council turned down his request because it judged that its publication might threaten the safety of the city by provoking its big neighbor, France. Next year, however, it was published in the French city of Lyon. For a detailed description of the process through which the book was published, see, Schelven, 62

CHAPTER III

THE EVANGELICAL VS. THE REFORMED ON SOCIAL REFORM

In this chapter we turn to some very recent explorations of the political dimensions of Calvinism. We will examine the contributions of Reformed thinkers to the discussions and debates that have occurred among North American evangelicalism regarding Christian social-political witness. These explorations are of special interest because they have been carried on within a framework of a strong commitment to biblical authority and to a conservative theological perspective, and they are presented as self-conscious attempts to apply traditional Calvinism to twentieth century political realities.

An explanation of the terminology to be used here is necessary at the outset. Our use of the term "evangelical" will designate a transdenominational North American Protestant movement that has been strongly influenced by pietist revivalism—thus placing a central emphasis on the transformation of individual "hearts." Not all Christians who identify with this evangelical movement endorse the thoroughgoing individualism that has often been associated with evangelicalism. But for our purposes here we will use the "evangelical" label to refer to people whose standpoint is strongly pietistic and individualistic.

The thinkers to whom we apply the "Reformed" label here themselves identify closely with the larger evangelical movement. But they have been critical of the almost exclusive emphasis on "personal" Christianity that has regularly typified the evangelical movement. Several of these writers (Stephen Monsma, Richard Mouw, Lewis Smedes and Nicholas Wolterstorff) stand in the tradition of an evangelically-oriented Dutch Calvinism; we will also make use of the works of two Calvinist-type Anglicans (Paul Marshall and John Stott) and even a Methodist (Stephen Mott) who takes a Reformed position on social-political questions.[1]

Regarding the issue of Christian social-political witness, the pietistic evangelicals seem to be divided, again, into two groups. I would call them respectively the dualistic evangelicals and the individualistic evangelicals. With all their similarities an important difference is to be found between them: the former's concern is exclusively spiritual and other-worldly, whereas the latter's concern is not necessarily confined to soul and Heaven. That is, the former is seldom interested in social reform, while the latter recognizes its necessity. As a result the former does not suggest any strategy for social reform, but the latter has its own answers to social problems.

In the sense that the individualistic evangelicals have concern for the conditions of this world, they are similar to the Reformed Christians. The difference between them and the Reformed evangelicals is on the strategies they propose to achieve the goal of social reform. The individualistic evangelicals think that the only effective and legitimate Christian way of reforming society is through evangelism. They disparage the social-political approach to social reform on the grounds that the change of society does not lead to the change of individual hearts, which is the ultimate purpose of Christianity.[2] The Reformed evangelicals, on the contrary, believe that society can be effectively changed when the changed people devote themselves not only to the proclamation of the gospel but to social-political witness. They encourage politics and social action.

We will begin by respectively outlining some of the basic themes of the dualistic and the individualistic evangelical perspectives on society and politics. Then we will set forth in some detail the Reformed perspective as it has been presented as an alternative to the more dualistic and individualistic strand of evangelicalism.

Dualistic Evangelicalism's Perspective on Social Reform

According to the dualist's view, what truly matters for Christians is the eternal fate of their soul in the coming world. Things related to the affairs of this world are not worthy of our serious attention. The only thing all human beings should try to secure in this world is the salvation of their souls. Compared with the paramount importance of these spiritual things, physical and earthly matters are of little significance.

Perhaps influenced by Hellenistic philosophy, the dualistic evangelicals tend to think that for Christians to be concerned with the external circumstances is evidence of a poor spirituality and ungodliness. True Christians are indifferent to external conditions. No matter how adverse the physical conditions may be, Christians of strong faith can and should overcome them. In short, true converts do not care about the social environments. Therefore, its change is unnecessary for them.[3]

Some evangelicals' dualism is shown in their mode of understanding several principal Christian concepts, such as the Kingdom of God, salvation, and evangelism.

The Kingdom of God

The dualistic-pietist evangelicals understand the Kingdom of God as something that will not come true until "the new heaven and the new earth" come. They do not expect anything significant to be realized in this world. Since the Bible teaches that we have no continuing city here, we had better think of it to be "a mere antechamber to eternity."[4]

Some dualistic-pietist evangelicals' anticipation of the imminent return of Jesus Christ and the Millennium has reinforced their social apathy. If the second coming of Jesus Christ is near, it would be a waste of time for Christians to endeavor for the improvement of this world. Isn't it foolish to hang new curtains and rearrange the furniture when the house is on fire?[5] The only thing Christians should do in this situation is to rescue as many perishing human beings as possible.

Salvation

Dualistic pietist evangelicals understand the term 'salvation' only in terms of other-world. For them salvation means almost exclusively going to Heaven instead of Hell. It has little to do with the life in this world.

Sometimes the dualistic-pietist evangelicals posit a broader meaning of salvation. They extend its meaning to be a deliverance from the power of sin, particularly from personal sins. To be in the process of sanctification is what they call the present dimension of salvation. Still, the usage of the word 'salvation' is confined to the personal dimension of morality. It is seldom mentioned with regard to the physical and social dimension.

The dualistic-pietist evangelicals can be said to be the most conservative group among evangelicals with regard to the social-political issues. Simply ignoring the necessity of social reform, they do not attempt to provide any strategy for it. They are convinced that saving souls by preaching the gospel is the only important task to which they are commissioned.

Evangelism

Dualistic-pietist evangelicals' understanding of 'evangelism' is seriously limited: they tend to think that evangelism is carried on only in words. In Mouw's phrase, evangelism for them is "a straightforward proclamation of the gospel" or "the verbal articulation of the biblical message." That is why they often claim to have been saved simply "to tell others."[6] If the salvation of the soul is the only and the most important thing in this life, and if people can be saved by hearing and believing the Gospel, they ask, why would we spend our time, energy and material for other than preaching the message of the Gospel in verbal forms? It would be foolish, they think, to waste our resources for the improvement of mere physical conditions of our perishing neighbor. Dualistic pietist evangelicals seldom think about how Christian's loving action for the unbelievers' external conditions may help them accept the message of the Gospel.

Individualistic Evangelicals' Perspective on Social Reform

Some pietistic evangelicals do not completely agree with the dualistic evangelicals' standpoint on social reform. Although they think that evangelism is the primary and the most urgent task Christians should assume, they nevertheless do not dichotomize body and soul, this world and the next world, the spiritual and the material, as much as their dualistic evangelical colleagues do. They appreciate the value of the body, this world and the material conditions for humans. So they admit to the necessity of social reform.

Regarding the strategy for reforming society, however, these evangelicals think the only and best way to do it is through evangelism. Directly addressing societal issues, they insist, is not the best means for bringing about social reform. A strong individualism characterizes their view of the relationship between individuals and society, salvation, church, and politics.

Individualistic View of a Human Being and Society

Individualistic evangelicals assume that the basic component of society is an individual, who is complete and self-sufficient apart from society. The only incentive for individuals to gather together as a society, they consider, is self-interest, or the desire to attain certain individual goods.[7]

Individualistic evangelicals view each human as a free and responsible being. They reject the liberal view of a human being as a helpless victim incapable of directing his/her destiny. This view of a human being with God-given ability and freedom to determine his/her own destiny promotes a tendency to help individuals help themselves rather than to change social structures.[8]

In the individualistic evangelicals' view, only the individual is responsible for his/her conditions in this world or in the next. Our predicament is the result of our own self-chosen idleness, inability or unbelief. Our social circumstances are not to be blamed.

Evangelism as a Strategy for Social Reform

According to the individualistic evangelicals' interpretation of the Bible and social reality, the source of all evil in the world is the heart of individuals. From the depraved nature of human beings flows every kind of sin. These personal sins are the true origin of all problems in society. Therefore, if we want to solve social problems, we should first solve the problem of sinful human nature. The change of individual hearts is the secret of social reform. How, then, can we change the individual hearts? It is possible only by presenting the verbal message of the Gospel to individual human beings. Nothing but evangelism can be an ultimate answer to the social problems. So long as individual hearts remain unchanged, whatever social, political and structural approach we make for social reform will fail, just touching the surface of the problem.

Individualistic evangelicals place much confidence in the individual's influence upon society. They are fond of those Bible stories that tell about what results from the heroic faith of individuals: Moses who led the millions of Israelites out of Egypt; David who defeated the giant Goliath; Daniel and his friends who triumphed gloriously by faith in God; the Apostle Paul who evangelized half of the world almost by himself. In fact, they could find in the Hebrews chapter 11 an impressive list of individuals who exerted an enormous influence on history by their great faith.

The individualistic evangelicals feel that the effectiveness of evangelism for social reform has been well-proved by modern precedents. They like to tell "often simple and always pointed" stories of Christian individuals who achieved an undeniably remarkable success in transforming their environment, such as a prison camp, the back streets of New York, or the country music circuit.[9] Encouraged by these stories, individualistic evangelicals often assume that the social environment has little influence on individuals. As Stephen Mott observes, they see the "influence flowing in only one direction," overestimating the influence of the individual upon the environment while underestimating the influence of the environment upon the individuals.[10]

In their exclusive emphasis on the power of evangelism for social reform, individualistic evangelicals have tended to undervalue or even ignore social action and political witness as distracting and secular. Even when they have acknowledged the necessity both of evangelism and social action, they do not consider the latter as important for social change as the former.[11]

Individualistic evangelicals' insistence on evangelism as a strategy for social reform is closely related to their understanding of several key Christian concepts such as salvation, sin, church as well as politics.

Salvation

Unlike the dualistic evangelicals who understand salvation as only "going to Heaven," individualistic evangelicals proceed to interpret it as a deliverance from the present misery in this world. Since they are aware that all the suffering on earth is the curse of sin, salvation from sin should include the removal of the curse of sin here and now. Even then, however, their discussion of human misery and deliverance from it stops at the individual level. That is, they think that they can help the suffering neighbor by their works of charity. A personal act of love, they often think, is enough. Approaching the solution of human suffering through politics or social action is usually beyond their consideration.

Ecclesiology

Pietistic evangelicals tend to emphasize the separateness of God's people. As the original meaning of the Greek *ecclesia* shows, they point out, the church is God's holy people called out of this world. The more separate from the world they are, the more sacred their states. They often understand the 'separateness' as a spacial concept, not so much as a style of life, or a value system. They think only what take place inside the church building is the function of the church: worshipping God, having fellowship, and building up each other. They think that, beyond evangelism, Christians have little to do outside the church.

Sin

Pietistic evangelicals tend to identify sin with very personal evil acts such as stealing, murder, adultery, gambling, profanity, desecrating of Sunday and lasciviousness. They are not often as sensitive to the existence and harmful result of social sin as to that of personal sins.

The Evangelical Attitude toward Politics

Some pietistic evangelicals view politics as double dealing, lying or at least shading the truth for the purpose of procuring some partisan advantage. Put sarcastically, it is a "strife of interests masquerading as a contest of principles, the conduct of public affairs for private advantage."[12] For others, politics is a strange world that they do not know how to go about influencing.

Seeing that the patterns of domination and manipulation characterize present political activity, pietist evangelicals conclude that the essence of politics is power and manipulation. The motive for anyone to become interested in politics, they suspect, is his/her ambition to gain and wield power.[13] The desire to dominate others, of course, is unchristian.

Some evangelicals, particularly those from the pacifist Anabaptist tradition, think of politics purely in terms of coercion. For them, government and law, which necessarily involve authority, force, and the threat of force are not compatible with a higher Christian calling to be a "suffering servant." They believe that Jesus exemplified the suffering servant by eschewing force even to the point of suffering injustices. The Crucifixion was the culmination of Jesus' way of accepting "powerlessness." To follow the path of Jesus Christ, Christians also should refuse to manage society by the use of political power.[14] They find it unnatural for Christians to seek and seize political power which is usually used to force their view of justice on others.[15]

The Reformed Perspective On Social Reform

Validity in the Individualistic Evangelical's Argument

Reformed thinkers acknowledge that a significant truth undergirds the evangelical's assertion that conversion brings forth social as well as personal consequences. Church history provides abundant evidence that evangelism has been conducive to social reform. When revival and spiritual awakenings were widespread in a society, movements for social reform followed almost without exception. In his *Revivalism and Social Reform in Mid-Nineteenth Century America*, Timothy Smith demonstrated the close relationship between the revival and the movements for social action in the 1850s.[16]

Reformed Christians are aware that the order of society is fragile if its members are without personal resources for morality. Carl Henry is correct at least in this point: in the absence of moral persons who are willing to do good, no body of law, however just, is sufficient to secure a good society. Legislative and judicial processes, though vitally important for social reform, are only the tip of the iceberg. The inner conformity to the command of the law cannot be achieved through mere structural rearrangement. Evangelism and Christian nurture provide the best motivations unthwarted by selfishness. Personal virtue is indispensable for the maintenance of social health.[17]

Even non-Christian scholars acknowledge the necessity of personal ethics for social justice. Erich Fromm, despite his great sympathy with Karl Marx, pointed out a weakness in the latter's neglect of the moral factor in human beings.

> Just because he assumed that all the goodness of man would assert itself automatically when the economic changes had been achieved, he did not see that a better society could not be brought into life by people who had not undergone a moral change within themselves. He paid no attention, at least not explicitly, to the necessity of a new moral orientation without which all political and economic changes are futile.[18]

The personal virtues, in turn, that constitute the prerequisites for the building of a just and humane society are not to be secured by coercion from outside. As Mott indicates, the formation of such personal qualities as self-respect and self-acceptance, tolerance, mutual respect, unselfishness, honesty, the sense of right and duty, the desire for equal treatment, and fidelity to law cannot, and indeed should not, be subject to governmental control. Politics alone falls far short in its attempts to create such values. From a Christian point of view, evangelism and Christian community make a necessary contribution to the process.[19]

Reformed scholars admit that evangelism also contributes. to the promotion of social justice by producing social activists. Since people are God's channel of justice, we cannot reasonably expect social justice to be promoted where the number of committed Christians constantly diminishes.[20] When social action is not accompanied by evangelism, those who previously suspected that Christian social activism might originate from a mere humanitarianism will firmly remain at the stage of applying their Christian faith only to the personal dimension of life.[21]

The Limits of Evangelism for Social Change

Granting the significance of evangelism in social reform, Reformed thinkers also point out that evangelism nontheless has its limits in establishing a just social order. In conquering evil in the individual heart, evangelism and Christian nurture play a decisive role. To deal with evil in society, however, another approach is needed. Reformed scholars observe that serious defects exist in the pietist evangelicals' perspective on the following points.

Individualism

Reformed thinkers observe that the conviction of the pietist evangelicals that the human unit is the individual makes it impossible for them to deal adequately with the predicament of human groups. Calvinistic evangelicals have tended to see the individual in terms of his social nature. Here what is basic to society is not the individual as such, but the various social spheres; thus, society is "a whole made up of individuals who are grouped into innumerable organic associations."[22]

Reformed thinkers seldom posit any radical discontinuity between the Old Testament and the New Testament. Unlike some evangelicals, they do not see, as Mouw puts it, any such "a shift from a primary concern with a corporate body in the Old Testament to a primary emphasis on the individual's relationship with God in the New Testament." The New Testament, like the Old, refuses to see a human being as isolated from his/her fellow humans.[23] Instead, it teaches that an individual Christian is a member of the body of Christ.

Reformed Christians readily admit that we search in vain in the New Testament for specific directions for social reform because the New

Testament writers do not directly call the structures into question. They insist, however, that many passages in the New Testament provide a basis for social ethics. The apostle Paul exhorted the Galatians to "do good to all people" as they had opportunity (Gal. 6:10). If social action is done for the purpose of doing good to some people, why should we shy away from it? If, as Jesus affirmed, to love our neighbor as ourselves is the Greatest Commandment, do we not sometimes find it necessary for us to adopt political action to obey that commandment? Thus, Calvinists argue that the individualistic evangelicals fail to take into account the enormous social changes that have been made during the last two millennia.[24]

Reformed Christians see that individuals do not live as separate beings. On the contrary, most human activities are often done in groups. We eat, learn, work, play, and worship not only individually but collectively. The individual's dependence on society is far more than most of us are aware. For example, the individual depends decisively on society in his or her formation of value:

> We are socialized into the acceptance or the avoidance of majorethical issues. Our socialization reflects the moral conscience of others who share our position in society, and our ethical reasoning is shaped before we actually come to reflect upon life or make conscious moral decisions....In short, social life consists of group ways of thinking and acting in which every individual participant's decisions are but a small portion of the development of the whole.[25]

Reformed Christians recognize that social structures can shape persons as much as the latter shapes the former. Unjust structures may drive the individual to act unjustly. A bad social circumstance often hinders even the well-meaning Christian from living out Christian values. Likewise, a good environment can deter a bad person from doing evil.[26]

Optimism

Reformed thinkers see that an optimism underlies the individualistic evangelicals' confidence in evangelism as a strategy for social reform. Mott observes the evangelicals' optimism at two points.

First, regarding the numerical quantity of the conversions; individualistic evangelicals overestimate the number of conversions occurring in the world. In order for society to be changed by evangelization, the majority of society must be born again. But this is an unrealistic goal. As Martin Luther said, "...filling the world with real Christians....This you will never accomplish: for the world and the masses are and always will be unchristian."[27]

Nor does the Scriptural evidence support such optimism. Jesus was not sure that when he came again, he would be able to find faith on the earth (Luke 18:8). This means that only the Christian minority is to take the responsibility of social reform.

Second, regarding the character and ability of professing Christians: Reformed Christians sense that individualistic evangelicals are optimistic in assessing the extent of the convert's moral transformation. Evangelicals often forget that the regenerate do not and cannot always live according to what is expected from them. First of all, it is not that the converts automatically and immediately come to know that such and such specific evil exists in society. "Those whose good will has been cultivated exclusively within personal relationships are frequently blind to social injustice and to the suffering of those they do not meet."[28]

Some Christians may dislike being reminded of the existence of social evil. Once they hear about that, their conscience tells them that there is something they should do about it. Not wanting that feeling of responsibility, they consciously avoid being exposed to such unpleasant facts. They are interested only in enjoying the blessings they receive as Christians through church life. They are not only unable but unwilling to relate their faith to specific issues.[29]

As a result, too many "changed" people have not contributed to changing society. For instance, Mott points out, American Bible Belt conversions brought about no general change of attitude regarding racial segregation, and Northern Fundamentalist conversions failed to result in a more just relationship between classes of the industrial structure.[30] Rather, the so called converts have sometimes taken part in doing evil. Shamefully, as Lewis Smedes observes, church history is

> strewn with sad stories of regenerate men [and women] pressing with ugly manners toward absolutely wrong headed goals....regenerate men [and women] have done and are doing some stupid and harmful things with full assurance that they have 'revealed moral principles' behind them.[31]

Individualistic evangelicals have failed to take into account the common fact that the justified are still sinners.

Dualism

Physical and Spiritual: Reformed scholars find no biblical grounds for the dualism, namely, physical and spiritual, this and the next world, and secular and sacred. They think that Christians should be on their guard against an unthinking acceptance of the dualistic aspects of their Platonic legacy.

Although the pietist evangelicals view human beings chiefly in terms of soul, the Reformed theologians observe that the Scriptural doctrine of a human being is, in John Stott's phrase, "a body-soul-in community." A human being is

> not just souls (that we should be concerned exclusively for their eternal salvation), nor just bodies (that we should care only for their food, clothing, housing...), nor just social beings (....become entirely preoccupied with their community problems). They are all three.[32]

Reformed Christians point out that the evangelicals fail to grasp the fact that the person is a unity and the suffering of the body affects the whole person. The spiritual and the physical are interdependent and the individual's relationship with his environment is integral. That is the reason Jesus directed his concern for people's greatest need whether it was physical or spiritual. The human soul is not the only object of God's salvation. God wants to save a whole person which includes body.[33]

Nature and Religion: Reformed Christians find that the dualistic evangelicals limit the area of God's sovereignty. Like a certain Old Testament pagan tribe who considered Jahweh to be the god of the mountain and not of the field, they assume that God's sovereignty is confined to the church. The world is not God's realm.

> Our God is often too small because he is too religious. We imagine that he is chiefly interested in religion—in religious buildings (churches and chapels), in religious activities (worship and ritual), in religious books (Bibles and Prayer Books).[34]

The Reformed view of God is that he is the God over all the universe. He is the God of heaven and earth. He is God not only for the believers but for the unbelievers, regardless of whether the latter recognize it or not. His sovereignty reaches everywhere. He is the God of nature as well as of grace, of the "secular" as well as of the "sacred."[35]

Reformed Christians observe that the pietistic evangelicals fail to see that what the Bible emphasizes is not the so-called "religious" acts but obedience to God in everyday life.[36] They seem to overlook the Old Testament prophets' declarations: "Does the Lord delight in burnt offerings and sacrifices as much as in obeying the voice of the Lord?" (I Samuel 15:22); "I desire steadfast love and not sacrifice" (Hos. 6:6)(Mic. 6:8).

Reformed Understanding of Some Christian Concepts

In addition to the different view of evangelism as a strategy for social reform, Reformed Christianity distinguishes itself from pietistic evangelicalism in its understanding of several key Christian concepts such as salvation, Kingdom of God, church, evangelism and politics.

Salvation

Reformed thinkers understand salvation to imply the cosmic dimension. "Every aspect of human existence was affected by human sin."[37] In Mouw's phrase, the "pervasive power of sin" not only devastated individuals but deformed and twisted "the entire created order," including the political institutions.[38] Accordingly, in Reformed view, the salvation of Jesus should be and is cosmic. Every realm of human life, including politics, can be redeemed by Jesus Christ.

Kingdom of God

Today it has come to be widely accepted that the Kingdom of God has two dimensions: the dimension of "now and here" and that of "not-yet." That is, the Kingdom of God has both present and futuristic character.

The Reformed Christians readily admit that the Kingdom of God is not identical with just social structures, but they know that it does not exclude them either. They know that a concern for the present dimension of the Kingdom does not necessarily cause a weakening of concern for the futuristic dimension of the Kingdom. Rather, they believe that seeking first the Kingdom of God involves trying in every possible way to eradicate the evil in this world.[39]

Reformed Christians do not find a radical discontinuity between the life in this world and life in the next. They think, therefore, that a new law that provides more justice for the oppressed is as essential a part of the

Kingdom of God as a heart born again. "Both are a sign and a foretaste of the promised re-creation of all things."[40] John Stott's definition of the Kingdom reflects the Reformed understanding. The Kingdom of God, he says, is

> God's dynamic rule, breaking into human history through Jesus, confronting, combating, and overcoming evil, spreading the wholeness of personal and communal well-being, taking possession of his people in total blessing and total demand....[41]

Evangelism

Reformed Christians are convinced that true Christian evangelism requires both word and deed. It consists of both loving our neighbor as ourselves and telling them how we have come to be able to do so.[42] As Mouw points out, in a personal confrontation, a zeal to preach the Gospel to another person is unauthentic if it is not accompanied by a genuine desire to know and meet his/her needs. Sometimes "nonverbal demonstration of concern and compassion" becomes an essential part of evangelism, for it helps the unbeliever to open his/her heart to hear the Gospel. In exactly the same way social action contributes to effective evangelism.[43]

Ecclesiology

Reformed scholars observe that the pietistic evangelicals seldom mention the church's "double identity," or "holy worldliness." The church is not only to be a holy people but a "worldly" people, in the sense that it is sent back into the world to witness and to serve. The church must keep both sides of its identity.

Mouw shows that even the classic Reformed ecclesiology has some flaw in this respect: the Belgic Confession (1566) stipulates the three marks of the true church as the preaching of the Word, the administration of the sacraments, and the execution of discipline. These, states Mouw, all concern "the internal life" of the institutional church. In other words, the traditional ecclesiology fails to account for the "body of persons in action in the world." Mouw suggests how integral ecclesiology can be worked out on the basis of the traditional ecclesiology: the church as a listening communiy must proceed to be a proclaiming community; the church served by Jesus Christ through communion must be willing to be servants in the world; disciplined by God's Word, it can become discipliners in the world.[44]

Jesus Christ did not fail to think of the church in its relation to and influence upon the world: You are the light of the world. A city set upon a mountain cannot be hidden (Matt. 5:14). Jesus chose twelve disciples not only for them to be with him but to go out and proclaim the Gospel and cast out the demons (Mark 3:14-15). The call of Jesus to discipleship was a call to a task.[45]

Reformed Christians insist that if the church is really the body of Christ, it must continue the incarnation. That is to say, Christians should not stop with preaching the gospel to the world. They should enter the world of misery and tragedy to identify themselves with the poor and the oppressed.[46] Stott reflects the Reformed understanding of mission when he defines mission to be:

> a whole life-style, including both evangelism and social responsibility, dominated by the conviction that Christ sends us out into the world as the Father sent him into the world, and that into the world we must therefore go—to live and serve, suffer and die for him.[47]

Structural Evil

Reformed thinkers observe that personal sin is not all that there is to sin. Scripture condemns as sin such social injustices as economic exploitation or oppression. When Isaiah called for the repentance of the Israelites, saying, "Come now, let us reason together...Though your sins are like scarlet, they shall be a white snow..." (Isa. 1:18), he was referring to the specific social evil of his time. The preceding verse makes this clear: "...seek justice, correct oppression; defend the fatherless, plead the widow" (Isa. 1:17).[48]

Reformed theologians emphasize that many of our greatest social evils are not so much the result of a conscious decision by individuals as they are the manifestations of culture and social order. There is an autonomous reality in them which works on its own laws. At the root of social injustices and problems there lurks structural evil which is rooted in society's prevailing socio-political or economic conditions.[49]

Monsma argues that structural evil is a pattern to the evil caused by structures or systems, a pattern formed by certain "attitudes or beliefs" like racism. It is part of the society's "culture." Political in nature, it is the evil flowing from "unjust laws or unjust law-enforcement systems." Monsma suggests two simple illustrations of structural evil: one is a person's cancer caused by a chemical company's improper disposal of industrial wastes, and the other is a parent's drinking problem which is brought on by unbearable, oppressive social and economic conditions.[50]

Mouw defines structural evil to be an "unjust kind of social system" in economic practices, laws, and prejudices. For instance, in the case of a Christian slum-dweller who rents from a Christian slum-landlord, the reconciliation they might experience together is severely hindered by the kind of social system in which they live. Mouw argues, therefore, that the formative influence of fundamental moods and attitudes perpetrated and reinforced by social practices, the mass media, and ethnic or economic bonds is not equal to "the sum of individual traits or opinions," and so cannot be dealt with adequately in one-to-one relationships.[51] That is why structural evil is not to be removed by merely changing individuals.

> ...institutionalization of the personal sinful project can come to have a life of their own. For this reason it is not enough to insist...that "changed hearts will change the society." If the manipulative patterns which are built into the very structures of social relationships are not changed, all of the effects of sin have not been challenged—and it may be that as a result many "hearts" will not be capable of adequate "change."[52]

Reformed Christians believe that in order to effectively achieve the goal of social reform there must be a sense of structural evil. We cannot simply depend on the individual act of love in each situation. One may take loving actions in an evil society, for example in a slave society. But if the order of society is unjust, the individual act of love becomes less meaningful.[53]

The Political Component of Today's Crucial Issues

Due to the existence of structural evil Reformed Christians believe that it is inevitable to use political means for social reform. The most critical social issues have such a strong political dimension that if we exclude a political approach to social evil, our ability to positively affect those issues will be seriously limited.

Monsma presents a striking example of this: one of the basic causes of the abject poverty of many of the third-world countries is the political and economic policies of powerful Western nations, including the United States. In order to perpetuate the profit of American corporations, American government has opposed and obstructed the emergence of the reformist governments in the third-world countries.[54] This should demonstrate that caring about the poor and hungry of the world cannot but involve a large measure of political action.

Reformed evangelicals criticize pietistic evangelicals for merely dealing with the symptoms of structural evils. In this way, we cannot treat the evils themselves. It is only by being involved in politics that we can attack the evils themselves. If Christians refuse to do this, they will be contributing to the consolidation of evil social, economic, and political patterns, and as a result many people will continue to be victims.[55]

Nature of Politics

It is true, Reformed thinkers admit, that our actual human politics is polluted by the elements of coercion and manipulation. But they are not its original or essential properties. They are to be seen as the "fallen" condition of politics originated from the first humans' rebellion against God. They are, in Mouw's words, a mere "perversion of an order that was a part of the original creation."[56]

Mouw does not agree with the pietistic evangelicals' argument that in the Garden there was no such thing as government or politics since restraint was not necessary there. Such a statement is sustained if government and politics are essentially matters of coercion instituted by God as a remedy for evil.[57] However, states Mouw, if we view the essential properties of politics as patterns of authority, accountability, collective decision-making, and corporate responsibility necessary for community life, we can find that in the Garden something existed that could be properly called a political order. We can visualize, Mouw suggests, a small community in the Garden constituting a theocracy. There, God was the governor over Adam and Eve, who in turn ruled over the animals. Thus, there was a kind of politics in the Garden. The reason there was no civil government in the Garden was not because there was no need of remedy for evil but because there were extremely small numbers of humans there.[58]

Mouw suggests another illustration to counter the pietistic evangelicals' argument that politics is a necessary evil introduced only after the Fall as a remedy for human sinfulness. He asks us to envisage a perfectly innocent community of saints, all members of which are without any sinful desire. Naturally, for the sake of corporate worship of God, they will need to set a time when the entire community gathers for worship. As it is improbable that all want exactly the same time for worship, they will have to discuss and decide when will be the most appropriate time for all. This very process of decision-making is a political activity, in which coercion and manipulation is not present.[59]

Reformed Christians are not unaware that politics is often misused for the private advantage of the ruling elite. That should not be the reason we reject politics as such. We should not commit the error of defining something by its misuse. We need to distinguish between "engaging in actions that will have the effect of coercing" others and "acting out of a desire to coerce and dominate" them.[60] Jesus' saying that one can be in the world but not of the world holds for the political world too. Reformed Christians consider that government and politics are institutions which are by nature good but have fallen. They have been ordained by God as his agents of justice and order in this world. There is nothing "inherently evil" about them.[61]

Force and Authority

Reformed scholars observe that some pietistic evangelicals still avoid politics and government because they confuse force with authority. Force is naked physical power, while authority is legitimate power supported by justice or morality. Force itself is neutral in value. Its value depends upon how and for what it is used. The essential element of authority is rightness or moral appropriateness. What governments exercise is not mere force or coercion but authority backed by force or coercion. Thus, Monsma defines the authority of government as "the rightful ability to command the obedience of another individual in a particular situation in order to achieve a particular goal or result."[62]

Some pietistic evangelicals wonder how the Sermon on the Mount and the instructions in Romans 13:1-7 can be compatible. They find the former prohibiting retaliation by force, while the latter authorizes it. This difficulty is easily resolved, however, when we observe that the apostle Paul makes a distinction between personal action and authorized political action.[63] What is forbidden to private citizens is authorized for the rulers.

The former are commanded not to take revenge but to leave room for God's wrath (Rom. 12:19), while the latter is "an avenging servant of God for wrath upon the doer of evil" (Rom. 13:4). Besides the Sermon on the Mount, many Scriptural passages seem to command Christians not to resort to force for retaliation but bear the injustice done to themselves. But these passages should not be taken as applicable to those people who justly exercise the authority given to them.[64] The Bible justifies and even requires of public officials to use force for public justice and welfare, whereas it bans the private person's use of force for vengeance. Or in Mott's words, "Love for the evil doer will always prohibit the ruler from retaliating for his or her own self-interest; love for others in the community, however, will call on the ruler to punish the evildoer."[65] Monsma gives an example of this: a Christian judge whose wife has been murdered would be required as a husband to forgive the murderer, but as a judge—if he has to judge the accused murderer—to apply to him/her the principle of justice.[66]

Imitatio Christi

While Anabaptist evangelicals argue that Christians, imitating Christ, should avoid the use of power, Reformed Christians think that the theme of *imitatio christi* ought not to be indiscriminately applied. They sense that the Crucifixion must be understood in terms of the unique mission of the Son of God. Jesus surrendered to death not because he condemned the use of power but because it was God's way of redeeming humankind.[67] Jesus' Crucifixion was a unique incident in the history of humankind intended for the divine-human. God did not intend it to be a normal mode of human action in their communal life. Since then, no human being has been, and will be commissioned with the task of redeeming the world in the same way as Jesus'.

Anabaptistic evangelicals should try to imagine, the Reformed thinkers argue, what would have happened if Jesus had used all the power he could mobilize to save his life from the Roman officials. Would there remain any chance of salvation for us?

> It is a false judgment to press the imitation of Christ in this connection and to contend that because Jesus was not directly politically involved Christians

should avoid politics....the theme of imitation is not to be interpreted literally, otherwise it would result in absurdities.[68]

Government: God's Answer to Structural Evil

Where does politics usually take place? If not all power relations are political, where does politics find expression? Reformed scholars understand that the political has to do with matters relevant to the actions of governments. Politics, argues Marshall, is what governments are, what they do or should be doing, and what we do in relation to them.[69] Politics is channeled through governments. We cannot think of politics apart from governments.

According to the Reformed understanding of government, God has instituted government through Jesus Christ. As the apostle Paul writes, "Thrones or dominions or principalities or authorities—all things were created through him and for him...in him all things hold together" (Col. 1: 16-7). The authority of government is from Jesus Christ to whom all authority on heaven and earth is given.[70]

Wherever the New Testament speaks of governing authorities it also mentions the specific task for which they have been given their authority. Of course, the basic task entrusted to government is the maintenance of the social order: governors are sent by God "to punish those who do wrong and to praise those who do right" (1 Peter 2:14). Rulers are "the servant of God to execute his wrath on the wrongdoer." (Romans 13:3-4).

Reformed Christians note, however, that the function of the government does not stop with the negative task of restraining evil. The Bible makes it clear that government has a positive role to play, namely, promotion of justice and fighting against oppression, (Deu. 16:18-20, Isa. 10:1-2, Eze. 45:9, Amos 5:12, Hab. 1:3-4, Ps. 1:2, 4, Rom. 13:3-4). On the basis of this account of the role of government, Reformed Christians believe that government is "God's answer to structural evil." It is the only institution that has the ability to confront and solve problems on a structural level. "Government alone," Monsma declares, "has the potential to make mandatory rulings that overturn evil structures and replace their evil with righteousness": only it can make binding decisions for all other institutions, groups and structures in society and back up its decisions with force, such as the police officer's gun, the prison cell, and the fine. This is precisely the role God intends government to play in society.[71]

Since government occupies such a vital position in God's strategy for social reform, Reformed Christians believe that God calls Christians to play leading roles in the government. As people who know what the original state of politics is, Christians have the duty of "redeeming" politics in the name of Jesus Christ.[72] Pietistic evangelicals who oppose Christian political involvement should insist, if they want their argument to be consistent, that nobody should be engaged in politics. As Monsma states:

> If a person truly believe that men and women ought not to be directly engaged in political activity... his or her consistent witness to those in political office can be to call them to abandon this work and take up other pursuits. To do otherwise would be the same as calling a prostitute not to abandon her profession but to serve God as a prostitute.[73]

Government, Justice, and Human Rights

If the task of government given by God is the execution of justice, what is justice? The classic definition of justice is "giving all persons their due." Reformed thinkers understand that justice means giving something its "right, its created place in God's world."[74] So the discussion of justice leads to the discussion of "rights." If we want to understand how government is supposed to do justice, the scope of the people's right must be determined first.

In order to determine what is due to people in relation to government, we need to discuss the human's place in God's creation. The Scripture tells us that humans are creatures made in the image of God. On the basis of this understanding of humanity, the Reformed theologians believe the scope of human rights to be very comprehensive. Monsma proposes that as image-bearers of God, human beings have rights "to be free, loving, creative, joyful beings, living lives of praise to God and service to others." A just order, therefore, means "societal customs, traditions, and laws that protect basic freedoms and assure a broad range of opportunities" including education, travel, the arts, and recreation.[75]

Mott proposes a variety of fundamental human rights based on the Scriptures: the sanctity of life; the right not to be permanently deprived of land; equality in the means of livelihood and where this is not possible, equality of opportunity; the right to rest from work one day in seven; the right of a servant of God not to be the servant of anyone else; the right to be protected from the arbitrary exercise of power; equality before the law or equal subjection to the law of all classes.[76]

Lewis Smedes contends that for persons to be properly treated as the bearers of God's image, every human should possess the right to provide decently for his family and the right of private and wholesome housing without which family life is not possible. In addition, the aged and poor should have the right to adequate medical care. For Smedes, these are rights rather than "matters of benevolence." If they are rights, he argues, the government has an obligation to at least try to secure them for every person.[77]

If these are the human rights, if to give everyone his/her own rights is justice, and if the task of government is to do justice, how can Christians make government do its duty of doing justice? What channels can we use to assume our responsibility for justice?

The Options for Social and Political Involvement

Reformed scholars suggest several levels of political involvement for social reform: as an individual, as a group, as a local church and as a denomination. We will note here some of the practical strategies proposed by Reformed writers.

As an Individual

Prayer: A Christian who does not pray and insists only on political action may well be suspected as a mere humanitarian, or at most, a believer of a weak faith. On the contrary, we must also beware that prayer should not be misused as a way of escape from social concern.[78]

Charity: this is a personal act of love. No doubt, it is a necessary and deeply meaningful form of Christian service to minister directly to the poor, the sick, the old, the handicapped, and the lonely by bringing them food, clothing, shelter, healing and comfort in Christ's name. Historically, it is well known that Christians are the people who have made great strides in such fields of charity work as city rescue missions for the outcast, homes for the aged, orphans, widows and unmarried mothers, emergency relief for disaster victims, schools for the blind and mentally retarded.

One thing to be noted regarding the role of charity as a means for social change is that the philanthropy of benevolent individuals cannot be the only or perfect solution to the social problems of our time.[79] As is the case with prayer, charity should not be an excuse to escape from doing more good which we can do. If we truly love our neighbors, we will not hesitate to take every lawful action on their behalf. Monsma introduces three levels of political involvement by an individual: citizen participant, citizen activist, professional activist.

Citizen Participant: All Christians should be politically active at least by being interested, participating citizens. The first step to be .a good citizen participant is to stay generally informed about politics: by knowing, for example, the names of the national and local elected officials and by having a general knowledge of the contemporary key issues on national and local levels.

Christians can share in public debate, vote in elections, sign a petition being circulated, and attend meetings called to educate the public on a particular issue. Furthermore, they can write to a public official or a newspaper, lobby a member of Parliament or Congress, take part in a demonstration, and belong to groups that are politically involved, for example, a labor union, an educator's organization, Amnesty International, consumer protection.[80]

Citizen Activist: Individual citizens can also play an active role in politically oriented groups, political parties, or candidate's campaign organizations. Although they do not have full-time, paid positions or hold public office, devoted citizen activists can exercise an enormous influence on the political system because most people are indifferent to politics. It is more so because of the tendency of the system to respond far more swiftly to pressures from groups than from individuals.[81]

Professional Activist: Undoubtedly, to hold a public office is "the most direct, immediate, and commanding" way to influence public policies. The professional politician, however, is not made in a day. It is impossible and undesirable that a citizen who has shown no concern for the public issues in his or her small town suddenly comes out to take a public office one day. To be able to make politics a profession, one needs at least to be active in one's community and its groups and organizations.[82]

As a Local Church

Local churches have a vital role to play in Christian political service. Mott shows three ways in which a local church can contribute to social change. The first is through various forms of social action and service. The second is to support and empower the individuals involved in mission by praying for them. The third is through the impact which the nonconforming life of the church has on the surrounding community.[83]

Mott insists that the local church should be a "parallel structure," which discloses the moral bankruptcy of the society around it and points to a new reality and new possibilities. It should ask questions that have not been asked, and challenge commonly held assumptions. By so doing it helps create alternative norms and values.[84]

Mouw maintains that the local church should embody the patterns for community life that God desires for all of human society.

> ...part of the calling of the people of God is to demonstrate in their life together it is possible for men to live, cooperate, and make decisions with one another in an atmosphere of trust, openness, mutual service, and hope....,and point to their own life together as a model of communal harmony based on collective obedience to the will of God.[85]

The function of the local church as a parallel structure, however, is not the only role it can play for social change. The demonstration of an alternative community is only one way to the goal. Local churches can also get involved in other sorts of social ministries.

Local churches can diversify their concern and action through groups. These groups can be composed of church members either of one local church, or several local churches. Christians who have particular social concerns in common can form groups in which they can study public issues of their interest. If necessary, on the basis of the result of their study, they can take appropriate action.[86]

Preachers

Can the preachers of the Word speak in the pulpit on social and political issues? If they can, to what extent? The Reformed scholars believe that good preaching is the first of Christian political services that local churches can offer. The pulpit must be a place to proclaim divine principles of justice as a part of the whole counsel of God. As a person who has been entrusted with the Words of God, the preacher is responsible for applying them to social and political issues.

One of the reasons that the preacher cannot avoid speaking on public issues is, as Mouw points out, that it is practically impossible to separate the message of personal ethics from the criticism of social structures. If a preacher really wants to preach nondiscriminating love of one's neighbor, it will be very natural to address the problem of discriminatory employment practices.[87]

The Reformed understanding of preachers is that they are ordained by God with the mission of guiding the life of God's people by God's Word. Therefore, if they are convinced that what they want to preach is not merely their own words and concerns but God's words and concerns, they can touch on political issues in the pulpit.[88]

As a Denomination

The problem of whether or not it is appropriate for the institutional church to issue official statements on public issues will be discussed in detail in chapter six.

Something More Important than the Result

Some evangelicals are unwilling to be politically involved on the ground that human attempts cannot achieve any significant progress in social reform until the return of Christ.[89] They say, "The redemption of the world doesn't hang on politics," or, "Total redemption depends upon a power outside ourselves."

It is true that success is not guaranteed for all Christian political actions. On the contrary, as Marshall affirms, "From the Constantinian hope of a Christian Empire, to the Puritan 'city set on a hill' in New England...the history of Christendom is littered with failed political dreams." Such a historical record, however, should not cause us to conclude that it is of no use to attempt any socio-political project. Despite a pessimistic prospect of the fruits of our efforts, we should undertake our task in this area. As Mouw puts it:

> The Christian is not called to launch programs that are successful in terms of human criteria. The Christian is called to be faithful to the heavenly vision. Thus, even if we could be certain that we live in an age in which the smallest degree of political success is impossible, this would in no way cancel our obligation to witness faithfully to the full triumphs of Christ's atoning work.[90]

Nor do we have to despair that our Christian political witness will always be of no avail. With God's blessing our social action might achieve a considerable success in reforming society. Of course only God can achieve a complete success in the work of social as well as personal salvation. But God seldom does these works in the vacuum. He works through human agents.

Political Neutrality and Status Quo

Some evangelicals insist that Christians should remain neutral in political affairs. In many cases, however, those who claim to be politically neutral are actually supporting the status quo.[91] The persons who refuse to be involved in politics nevertheless have political impact. Such inaction tends to support existing policies and personalities.[92] In Paul Henry's words, "Even utter silence on political questions was a political statement of approval or at least acquiescence." Henry considers that the church's silence is either a kind of cowardice or a policy of the status quo. In his judgement, church leaders who avoid speaking on public issues in the name of separation of church and state are well aware that they are on the side of the status quo.[93] They are not at all consistently apolitical. While denouncing the political radicalism, they pray at the breakfasts of unjust dictators.[94]

Because no one is outside the texture of economic and social life, no one can completely avoid responsibility for it. In this area of life "inaction is a kind of action."[95] Especially in an oppressive society, the silence of the church cannot but be taken as a countenance of the existing regime, avoiding its responsibility to defend the oppressed:

> We are already involved merely by virtue of living in God's world. if we try to be passive or to ignore what is happening about us, then we are merely saying that we accept the way things are as being the way God wants them to be. If we try to be passive we are, in fact, expressing political views for we are accepting the situation as it is. Given the sin and suffering in the world such a political stance can only be viewed as sub-Christian, a turning away from what God and our neighbor ask of us. To be Christian we must take up our political responsibility and act in a way that moves governments to do justice.[96]

Some people worry about a "seduction" of the church by the cause of social concern. But the profession of "neutrality" also can be a sign of seduction as the church is seduced by materialism and hedonism.

Christians can be so comfortable and satisfied in this world that they cannot find any reason to risk conflict.[97]

Without concern for others, loyalty to religion is nothing but "a pious indolence" which abandons its responsibility for this miserable world and seeks only to rescue its own virtue.[98] Christian apathy toward politics can be an expression of unconcern about suffering neighbors who are anxiously waiting for justice. To refuse to act on one's belief is to neglect a God-ordained means for the restraint of structural evil.[99]

1 Dr. Mott has assured me that he agrees with my characterization of his thought as falling within the Reformed tradition. Indeed, his forthcoming work, *A Christian Understanding of Political Thought* (Oxford University Press, 1993), makes even more extensive use of Calvin's political theology than the work that I am citing here.

2 Carl F. H. Henry, "Evangelicals in the Social Struggle," *Christianity Today* 10 (October 8, 1965): 3-11, in Augustus Cerrilo, Jr. and Murray W. Dempster, ed., *Salt and Light: Evangelical Political Thought in Modern America* (Grand Rapids, Michigan: Baker Book House Company, 1989), 39.

3 Stephen C. Mott, *Biblical Ethics and Social Change* (Oxford University Press, 1982), 115.

4 Richard J. Coleman, *Issues of Theological Warfare: Evangelicals and Liberals* (Grand Rapids, Michigan: William B. Eerdmans Publishing Co., 1972), 203.

5 John R. W. Stott, *Involvement: Being a Responsible Christian in a Non-Christian Society* (Old Teppan, New Jersey: Fleming H. Revell Company, 1984), 35.

6 Richard J. Mouw, *Political Evangelism* (Grand Rapids, Michigan: William B. Eerdmans Publishing Co, 1973), 8, 76, 14.

7 *Ibid.*, 63-66.

8 Coleman, 176-177.

9 Robert Booth Fowler, *A New Engagement: Evangelical Political Thought: 1966-1976* (Grand Rapids, Michigan, William B. Eerdmans Company, 1982), 145-6.

10 Mott, 119-120.

11 Mouw, *Political Evangelism*, 8.

12 Ambrose Bierce, *The Devil's Dictionary* (Mount Vernon, New York: Peter Pauper Press, 1958), 48, quoted in Marshall, 11-12.

13 Mouw agrees that "all Christians should hope to be delivered from the latter pattern, since the desire to dominate and coerce is closely related to the sinful project that began with the serpent's lie, 'You shall be as gods.'" He adds, however, a warning that we should "make a distinction between engaging in actions that will have the effect of coercing other human beings and acting out of a desire to coerce and dominate others." Mouw, *Politics and the Biblical Drama* (Grand

Rapids, Michigan: William B. Eerdmans Publishing Company, 1977), 109.

14 For a discussion of Anabaptist theme of *imitatio christi,* see John Howard Yoder, *The Politics of Jesus* (Grand Rapids, Michigan: William B. Eerdmans Publishing Co., 1972), chs. 7-9. For a Reformed response, see Mouw, *Biblical Drama*, ch. 5.

15 Stephen V. Monsma, *Pursuing Justice in a Sinful World* (Grand Rapids, Michigan: William B. Eerdmans Publishing Co., 1984), 13; J. G. Davies, *Christians, Politics and Violent Revolution* (London: SCM Press Ltd., 1976), 33. Mott, 194-5, Mouw, *Biblical Drama*, 101,

16 Timothy L. Smith, *Revivalism and Social Reform in Mid-Nineteenth Century America* (New York: Abingdon Press, 1957). For the history of the evangelicals' rigorous activity for the social reform, see also Stott, vol. 1, ch. 1.

17 Carl Henry, "Evangelicals...," in *Salt and Light*, 29.

18 Erich Fromm, *The Sane Society* (New York, Rinehart, 1955), 264, quoted in Mott, 111-112.

19 Mott, 197-8.

20 *Ibid.*, 112.

21 *Ibid.*, 112.

22 Lewis B. Smedes, "The Evangelical and the Social Question," in *Salt and Light*, 57; Monsma, 52.

23 Mouw, *Political Evangelism*, 40.

24 Coleman, 187.

25 Mott, 13.

26 Coleman, 198, Lewis B. Smedes, "The Evangelical and the Social Question," in *Salt and Light*, 44.

27 Martin Luther, "Secular Authority: To What Extent it Should be Obeyed," J. Dillenberger, *Martin Luther, Selections from His Writings* (Doubleday, Anchor Books, 1961), 370-4.

28 Davies, 17.

29 Coleman, 197-198.

30 Mott, 114.

31 Smedes, "The Evangelical and the Social Question," in *Salt and Light,* 43-44. Mott shows good instances of this: Bible belt

conversions resulted in no general change with respect to racial segregation and Northern Fundamentalist conversions failed to result in more just relationships between classes of the industrial structure. Mott, 114.

32 Stott, *Involvement*, 41.

33 Coleman, 178-9, Mott, 115-118.

34 Stott, 37.

35 *Ibid*.

36 Davies, 14.

37 Paul Marshall, *Thine is the Kingdom: A Biblical Perspective on the Nature of Government and Politics Today* (Grand Rapids, Michigan: William B. Eerdmans Publishing Co., 1984), 37.

38 Mouw, *Political Evangelism*, 13, 15.

39 Davies, 21.

40 Isaac C. Rottenberg, "The Shape of the Church's Social-Economic Witness," in *Salt and Light*, 92.

41 Stott, 46-47.

42 Mouw, 14.

43 *Ibid*., 7, 77.

44 Mouw, *Politics and the Biblical Drama*, 57-59, 67-68.

45 Hendrikus Berkhof, *The Doctrine of the Holy Spirit* (Atlanta, Georgia: John Knox Press, 1964), 41.

46 Stott, 44-45.

47 *Ibid*., 36.

48 Mott, 17.

49 *Ibid*., 3-4, 11-12.

50 Monsma, 10-11.

51 Mouw, *Political Evangelism*, 15-17.

52 Mouw, *Biblical Drama*, 50.

53 Mott, 54.

54 Monsma, 26, 29. This is one of the reasons why an Anti-American movement took place in Korea since 1980. Before that, Korea was said to be one of the few countries where anti-American feeling did not exist. See, Nicholas Wolterstorff, *Until Justice and Peace Embrace* (Grand Rapids, Michigan: William B. Eerdmans Publishing Company, 1983), especially, ch. 1.

55 Monsma., 11, 12

56 Mouw, *Biblical Drama*, 35. The view of government as essentially "coercive" is an important ground for John Howard Yoder to argue that Christians ought not to participate in government. He treats the political realm as such a "necessary evil" that God introduced as a remedy for the human's fallen condition.

57 Gordon Clark, *A Christian View of Men and Things* (Grand Rapids; Eerdmans, 1952), 138, 146, quoted in Mouw, *Biblical Drama*, 32-3.

58 Mouw, *Political Evangelism*, 45; *Biblical Drama*, 33.

59 Mouw, *Political Evangelism*, 45-6.

60 Mouw, *Biblical Drama*, 109.

61 Monsma, 59.

62 Monsma, 17-8.

63 Marshall, 46.

64 Monsma, 19.

65 Mott, 184.

66 Monsma, 19.

67 Mott, 179-180.

68 Davies, 25.

69 Marshall, 11-12.

70 Ibid., 47.

71 Monsma, 19-21, 12.

72 *Ibid.*, 58.

73 *Ibid.*, 60.

74 *Ibid.*, 38; Marshall, 56; Mott, 53.

75 Monsma, 37, 40, 30.

76 Mott, 52.

77 Smedes, "The Evangelical and the Social Question," in *Salt and Light*, 46, 55-56.

78 Paul Rees, "Prayer and Social Concern," in *The Chicago Declaration,* ed. Ronald J. Sider (Carol Stream, Ill.: Creation House, 1974), 78-87.

79 Smedes, "Social Question," in *Salt and Light*, 55.

80 Monsma, 31, 85-8; Stott, 34.

81 Monsma, 89-92.

82 *Ibid.*, 92-93.

83 Mott, 131-135.

84 *Ibid.*, 136.

85 Mouw, *Political Evangelism*, 47.

86 Stott, 51, 34.

87 Mouw, *Political Evangelism*, 16.

88 *Ibid.*, 81.

89 *Ibid.*, 27-8.

90 *Ibid.*, 29.

91 Monsma, 83, 86; Davies, 30.

92 Monsma, 83.

93 Fowler, 155.

94 Mouw, *Political Evangelism*, 33.

95 N. Micklem, *The Theology of Politics* (Oxford University Press, 1941), quoted in Davies, 30.

96 Marshall, 64.

97 Fowler, 159.

98 Bonhoeffer, *Ethics*, SCM Press, 1955, quoted in Davies, 16.

99 Monsma, 86.

CHAPTER IV

CHURCH AND STATE IN KOREA (1884-1945)

The discussion of church and state in Korea from 1884 to 1945 confronts a somewhat different issue from that which is generally dealt with under that topic. In modern times, what is normally discussed under the topic of church and state presupposes that those two institutions are composed of the same people. In the case of Korea from 1910 to 1945, the situation was different: the members of the church were Koreans, but the government was ruled by other people, the Japanese. That is to say, in the discussion of church and state in Korea from 1884 to 1945, the issue of "nation" or "nationhood" must be necessarily highlighted. Therefore this chapter deals not with the issue of church and state as such, but mostly with the issue of what Korean Christians did for the cause of national independence and how they responded to Japan's imperialistic attempt to colonize their country.

Another point that should be kept in mind in dealing with this issue is that there did not exist a Korean church worthy of the name during the former part of this period. It was in the year 1885 that Protestantism was first introduced in Korea; in 1907, the independent Korean presbytery was constituted, and in 1912, after Korea's annexation to Japan, the Presbyterian Church of Korea was instituted as the first national ecclesiastical organization in Korea. In other words, we cannot expect too much socio-political impact from the Korean church in this period. As will be seen later, most Christian nationalistic actions in this period were taken by individual Christians, and not by the church as an institution.

Socio-political Actions of Early Korean Christians

The first Protestant missionaries in Korea entered into the country in the status of a teacher or a physician. They could not be admitted to Korea as missionaries. The first resident missionary to Korea was H. N. Allen. His official title was physician to the American legation in Korea.

Horace G. Underwood, the first clerical missionary to Korea, was known as an English teacher at a government hospital. They were sent by the Presbyterian Church in the U.S.A. Henry Appenzeller and William. B. Scranton, M. D. were from the Methodist Episcopal Church in America. Naturally they could not be engaged in direct evangelistic works. They had to be satisfied with indirect methods of evangelism, that is, education and medical service.

Accordingly, the number of converts as the fruit of their evangelistic work was insignificant. Going through national crises such as the Sino-Japanese War in 1894, the battlefield of which was Korea, and the Ulmi Incident in 1895 in which the Japanese brutally murdered the Korean queen Minbi, the Koreans felt so insecure that some of them came to the Christian church to seek refuge. Even at this time, however, the number of baptized Korean Christians in 1896 was only 777. 1897 statistics show that there were 5,000 Christians including 3,000 Presbyterians.[1] It would be unreasonable to expect that this small number of Christians could do much in terms of socio-political action.

During the last decade of the nineteenth century, Korean Christians' social action usually took the form of civil disobedience against the corruption of the magistrates. It was often expressed as a refusal to pay the taxes unjustly levied on them. Christian resistance to unjust taxation seems to have been widely known. An official who was appointed as a magistrate for a Northwest county in Korea petitioned the government to send him to another county. The reason for this petition was interesting: there were too many Christians in that region.[2]

Independent Club and Christians

After Japan defeated China in the 1894 war, Korea's fate was like a candle flickering in the wind. She could be colonized at any moment either by Japan or by Russia. At this time there arose among some Koreans a notable movement to secure the independence and modernization of Korea. The leader was Jaepil Suh, a Christian who studied and earned his M. D. degree in America. With the help of some Christian intellectuals and bureaucrats, he formed a club called the "Independents." To achieve their goal they made efforts to awaken the national awareness of Korean people, spread democratic ideas and hold public debates on political issues. They also criticized the corruption and the inefficiency of the government, suggesting policies for social reform through their newspaper, *Independence*. One scholar indicates that this was the last chance given to Koreans to secure the independence of their nation. If the government had accepted the suggestions of the Club and undertaken the plan for modernization, Korea might not have been so helplessly made into a colony of Japan within a decade or so.[3]

Missionaries and Politics

The Korean political situation in the 1890s and 1900s was so critical that it was not easy for the American missionaries to devote themselves to purely religious works. As Christian ministers who came to serve Korean people, it would have been strange for them to have completely distanced themselves from the issues that had a decisive influence on the people they claimed to serve. Naturally they tended to be sympathetic with the Koreans and tried to support the position of the Korean government. Apart from the human inclination to take the side of the weak, they could not successfully carry out their missionary work without securing the favor of the Korean magistrates, who were still suspicious and even antagonistic toward Christianity.

Because Dr. Allen cured a high Korean official, Min Young Ik, who was seriously wounded in 1884 coup, he was appointed a court physician. From this time on the relationship between the missionaries and the Korean court grew rapidly. The missionaries gained so much of the Korean king's confidence that when the King was trembling in panic after seeing the brutal murder of the queen by the Japanese, he called for the missionaries and had them stand guard over him every night.[4]

The nineteenth century and the first few decades of the twentieth were the age of imperialism. By 1880 Western powers had already colonized most Asian countries and were competing in Korea to secure as much profit as possible. Korea had a strategic importance for both Japan and Russia. For Japan, Korea seemed to be able to serve as a bridgehead for the invasion of China and the Asian continent. For Russia, in turn, she could provide many naval ports that were not frozen in winter. Korea was more attracted to Russia, because she desired to check the influence of Japan. What made the problem more complicated was that England and America were also interested in the Far East. For England especially, Korea was one of the strategic locations for deterring the southward advance of Russia. In the eyes of England and her friend America, Japan was a useful partner that could be used to check the expansion of Russia in the Far East. For this reason the British and American governments wanted Japan to have superiority over Russia in Korea.

Ironically, however, some American missionaries in Korea, apparently oblivious to the world strategy of their country, were endeavoring to help Korea to keep her independence by pursuing her own diplomatic policies, which were pro-Russian and anti-Japanese. This meant that unintentionally and unknowingly the American missionaries in Korea were working against the diplomatic policy of their own country. The disturbed American legation sent a message to these missionaries in the name of the Secretary of State. Unquestionably, it was intended to curb the missionaries' pro-Korean political actions:

> By direction of the Secretary of State I am required to make publicly known to each and every citizen of the United States sojourning or being temporarily or permanantly in Korea, the repeatedly expressed view of the Government of the United States that it behooves loyal citizens of the United States in any foreign country whatsoever to observe the same scrupulous abstention from participating in the domestic concerns thereof which is internationally incumbent upon his government. They should strictly refrain from any expression of opinion or giving advice concerning the internal management of the country, or from any intermeddling in its political questions. If they do so, it is at their own risk and peril. Neither the representative of this government in the country of their sojourn, nor the Government of the United States itself, can approve of any such action on their part, and should they disregard this advice it may perhaps not be found practicable to adequately protect them from their own consequences. Good American citizens, quitting their own land and resorting to another, can best display their devotion to the country of their allegiance and best justify a claim to its continued and efficient protection while in foreign parts, by confining themselves to their legitimate vocations, whether missionary work, or teaching in schools, attending the sick, or other calling or business for which they resort to a foreign country.[5]

Greatly embarrassed at the government's strong official expression of dissatisfaction with their political actions, and even the threat to withhold protection from the results of their action, American missionaries must have been discouraged from that moment from continuing to involve themselves in the political affairs of Korea.

In addition to pressure from the legation, American missionaries felt that Korean Christians were inclined to be too political. It was understandable to a great extent that these Christians were concerned about the critical situation of their country. The problem, however, was that the young Christians, newly converted, seemed to be so interested in the national issues that they tended to neglect their spiritual growth. Partly by the influence of the American legation, and partly afraid of excessive political orientation of Korean Christians, the Presbyterian Missionary Council decided to make a statement on the "Relationship between Church and State." Korean scholars agree that this was the origin of the "depoliticization" of Korean Church.

1. We the clergy are determined not to meddle in the political, and national affairs.
2. There exist treaties between Korea and our countries. We abide by the agreements in those treaties. The ecclesiastical affairs and the political ones are not identical. We have taught our people that we do not get together at church to treat the political affairs, neither is the church to interfere in them.
3. Koreans do not cease to be citizens of Korea even after becoming Christians. Therefore we exhort them to be loyal to the emperor without disobeying God's word, to obey the magistrates and to observe all the laws.
4. The church ought not to induce the individual Christians to participate in the party politics, nor ought it to dissuade them from doing so. The church is not responsible for the mistakes and violations they made during their political actions.
5. The church is not a place for politics, therefore, the church buildings and Christian schools are to be used for the cause of religion, not for the politics. Christians should not meet at church to discuss the political affairs, not to mention at the parsonage.

The first point was the clergy's determination to separate themselves from the political involvement. What is not clear here was whether they thought it appropriate for missionaries in a foreign country or for clergy in general. The second point connoted, however, their consciousness of being foreigners in Korea.

The third point concerned the relationship between earthly power and Christian responsibility to obey it. This also suggests that there were incidents where Korean Christians disregarded the legitimate commands of the magistrates and the laws of the state on the ground that they had become citizens of the Kingdom of Heaven.

The fourth point acknowledged that for Christians political activity was not wrong in itself. It was up to the individual Christian's decision whether or not to participate. It was not a matter for the church to encourage or discourage.

The fifth point reflects that Korean Christians often talked about politics and nationalistic issues at church or at the parsonage, and that the missionaries were annoyed by that.

Although this statement sounds pretty fair, it was not without problems. The most problematic was the second point which presupposed that the concerns of the church and of the state were always so clearly distinguishable from one another.

Korean Christians' Response to the Annexation

By defeating Russia in the Russo-Japanese War in 1904, Japan removed the last rival for the occupation of Korea. There was now no country which stood in the way. England had already consented to Japanese control over Korea in the 1902 British-Japanese Treaty for alliance and renewed it in 1905.[6] The United States also admitted the right of Japan to subjugate Korea on the condition that Japan should acquiesce in the American occupation of the Philippines.[7] Russia recognized Japan's "paramount right" in Korea in the Portsmouth Treaty, which was produced through President Theodore Roosevelt's initiative in September 1905.[8] Thus, in November 1905, the impatient Japan deprived Korea of all diplomatic rights, and finally, in August 29, 1910, annexed her.

How did Korean Christians respond to the decline and fall of their country to an imperialistic country? In 1905, there were about 10,000 baptized Christians and 30,000 catechumens in Korean Church. Even in 1907, after many new converts were added by the Great Revival, the number of the baptized Christians was still less than 20,000, and with around 100,000 catechumens.[9] Estimating the population of Korea in 1907 between fifteen million and twenty million, Christians were less than one percent of the whole population. Moreover, until 1907 there were no ordained Korean pastors. One cannot reasonably expect too much from this weak church. Nevertheless, Korean Christians took various actions at the moment of the national crisis.

The most common response was the holding of prayer meetings. In accordance with the decision of the Presbyterian Council, three hundred Presbyterian churches in Korea held meetings to pray for the country for a week, from the next day to Thanksgiving Day, 1905.[10]

Some Christians were not satisfied with prayer without action. Changho Ahn, Sunghun Yi, and Donghwi Yi thought that it was impossible for Korea to keep independence without enlightened and civilized people. Judging that education was the most urgent and effective way to lay the foundation for independence, they erected many private schools such as Daesung, Ohsan, and Bochang.[11]

Others formed political associations to achieve their goal of restoring the sovereignty of the country. The most famous of them was Shin Min Hoe, meaning "The New People's Association." This was formed in 1907 at the proposal of some national leaders such as Changho Ahn, Tuckki Chun, Dongwhi Yi, etc. One of their goals was to overturn the monarchy and establish a republic. To accomplish their purposes, Shin Min Hoe endeavored to awaken the Korean people's national consciousness through journalism, education, and public speeches, spreading Western democratic ideas and civilization to them. Shin Min Hoe also made economic efforts to raise the national wealth by founding an international trade company called Sang Mu Dong Sa.[12]

Some radical Christians resorted to terrorism. The most famous of those incidents was the assassination of Ito in 1909 by the cooperation of a Roman Catholic, Joonggun Ahn, and a Protestant, Yon-joon Uh. Ito was one of the major figures who played decisive roles in the modernization of Japan, making her one of the world powers. Recognized as the protagonist in making Korea Japan's protectorate in 1905, he was appointed the first Governor-General in Korea. He was assassinated just before the final annexation of Korea to Japan.

In 1908, another Protestant, Inhwan Chang, shot an American in San Francisco. His victim's name was Stevens, an advisor in the department of foreign affairs of Korea. As a pro-Japanese, he had infuriated Koreans by making a statement in a press interview that Koreans are not entitled to have a independent country.[13] Some Christians, including Jaemyong Yi and his friends, attempted in vain to assassinate Wanyong Yi, the prime minister of Korea who played the most positive role in handing over Korea to Japan.

The Attitude of the Missionaries between Korea and Japan

What was the Church's official position in this critical period between 1905-1910? It must be remembered here that until this time the Korean church was represented by the leadership of hundreds of missionaries, most of whom were American. It was in 1907 that the first seven Korean pastors were ordained.

What did the missionaries teach to Korean Christians on the issue of national independence? In fact, the missionaries were faced with a dilemma: if they taught the Korean Christians to resist the unjust invasion of Japan, they would have been immediately regarded as the enemy of Japan and would most probably have been expelled from Korea, since Japan was actually in control over Korea after 1905. On the other hand, if they exhorted Korean Christians to accept the control by Japan and submit to it, they would certainly be suspected as the agents of Japan and would lose the trust of Koreans. What could the missionaries do if they lost the confidence of the people?

After much consideration, they finally decided to choose neutralism or a non-committal stance as their official policy. Charles Allen Clark of the Northern Presbyterian Mission, writing from Seoul on February 15, 1908, said:

> As to the Board's action for a non-committal and neutral policy concerning political matters, it does not change by one iota our mission policy for it has always been rigidly held and enforced. More than any other mission in Korea we have insisted upon that policy and when one gets to the bottom of the whole matter, it is exactly because we have always maintained that policy that we stand today as we do before the Japanese. We believe that the church as a church has absolutely nothing to do with politics in any way....Our position has been that the church is a spiritual organization and as such is not concerned with politics either for or against the present or any other government.[14]

Here was a missionary taking pride in the fact that he and his fellows had not the least interest in the matter of the greatest concern to the people they claimed to serve. Eager to prove how much he had been apolitical, Clark set forth an ironic boast: "Literally hundred of times in the past we have stood by when our people have been suffering persecution and we have refused to speak one word to any magistrate that might free them...."[15]

The Methodist Episcopal Mission took the same stand. The remarks made by Bishop M. C. Harris represented the official position of this church:

> The Church in Korea occupied a delicate position. It is a great power, and during the troubles of last year, guided by the missions, it stood aloof from all

> disturbances and held the people in order....Our missionaries in Korea gave themselves absolutely and wholly to the work of evangelizing the people. They are not connected, directly or indirectly with any domestic or any political problems.[16]

This policy of the Methodist Episcopalian Mission was the response to the request which Ito made in 1905. Inviting Bishop Harris, Ito suggested a kind of division of roles between church and state, saying, "Let me deal with the political affairs in Korea, and I hope you take care of the spiritual sphere."[17]

The neutralism or non-committal stance towards the oppressor or the oppressed is, however, just another expression of supporting the status quo. It is a way of siding with the oppressor and taking part in the injustice. It never can be a genuine neutrality. Such was the case with the missionaries in Korea at that time. "As far as we can discover in the private letters of the missionaries," says L. George Paik who examined a vast amount of missionary materials of those times, "a large number favored and cooperated with the Japanese and made an effort to quiet the restlessness of the Christians."[18] They spoke not "a word" to the Japanese for the cause of Korea, while uttering numerous words for the cause of Japan. Wade Koons, a missionary from the Northern Presbyterian Mission, said in his letter of February 4, 1908:

> We have not opposed the Japanese....We have assured the people that their duty was to obey the Japanese and to do so with a 'sweet mind' and not to work for independence....I have spent hours explaining to the church officers and teaching men advantages of Japanese rule, and I cannot think of one who has been kept from it.[19]

Charles Allen Clark reported in the letter mentioned above: "One year ago the Wɨpyeng movement known as the Righteous Army began and it now continues. When it first began it spread like wildfire. We set ourselves rigidly against it and we have held our church...rigidly from going into it."

Koreans who had been thinking of the missionaries as the apostles of justice were greatly embarrassed to see that the missionaries took the side of Japan. Feeling betrayed, they began to suspect that the missionaries might be a vanguard of the imperialists, and Christianity "the handmaid of imperialism." Some Korean Christians simply left the church in anger.

More radical ones attacked the missionaries on the street; some even threatened their lives.[20]

Especially strong was the pro-Japanese tendency among the leading missionaries. It is understandable to some extent because they were not in a position to disobey directions from their mission boards in America which, in turn, must have been influenced by the foreign policy of the government.

Not all the missionaries, however, agreed with the policy of their superiors. Among the missionaries who spent most of their time with the people, there were not a few who were sympathetic with Koreans. The most positive among them was Homer B. Hulbert. After the Korean-Japanese Treaty of 1905 that made Japan a protectorate over Korea, but a few days before its effectuation, he visited the White House to see President Theodore Roosevelt and deliver the petition of the Korean emperor to him. The content of the petition was that the Treaty was invalid because it was made under the threat and violence of Japan and that America, in accordance with the treaty which they made with Korea in 1882, should try to rescue Korea from the Japan.[21] Neither the Korean emperor nor Hulbert had known that Theodore Roosevelt had already agreed that Japan would occupy Korea. Though the arrival of the Korean emperor's petition was announced to the President, it was not received until after the Treaty between Korea and Japan was effectuated. When it was found it was too late. Hulbert got angry and severely denounced the unfaithfulness of American government:

> Even while the whole Korean people were convulsed by the high-handed act of Japan, and some of the very highest Korean officials were seeking oblivion of their country's wrongs in suicide, the American Minister in Seoul was feasting the Japanese who had compassed the destruction of Korean nationality. Can it be wondered at that the feeling of confidence which Korea reposed in the friendship of America should have experienced a sudden and sharp reaction. Americans of every class had been telling Korea for a quarter of century that the American flag stood for fairness and honesty, that we had no purely selfish interests to subserve, but stood for right, whether that right was accompanied by might or not; but when the pinch came we were the first to desert her, and that in the most contemptuous way, without even saying good-bye.[22]

Hulbert even advised Koreans to resist Japan by force. A Korean newspaper reported his radical speech: "Although Japan is a world power, she will not be able to annihilate all of the twenty million Korean people. If Koreans rise up with the determination to fight against Japan to the end, Japan's financial resource will be exhausted within three years, and not a single Japanese will be seen in the territory of Korea."

Not all the missionaries were so radical as Hulbert, just as not all were so pro-Japanese as the missionaries in high positions. It would be fair to say that many missionaries took their position somewhere between Bishop Harris and Hulbert. Sympathetic as they were with Koreans, they acknowledged the political realities. To them, it seemed that Japan's occupation of Korea was irrevocable. The best way for Korea was, they thought, to accept the Japanese rule as an unavoidable reality for the time and to wait until she had developed the capacity to expel Japan and to restore her independence.

The Great Revival of 1907

Some mention seems necessary with regard to a very significant incident in Korean church history, the Great Revival in 1907. Begun in an annual Bible-study meeting at a Presbyterian church in Pyongyang, resulting in an unprecedented spiritual experience for Korean Christians as well as moral enhancement, the Great Revival has exercised a formative influence on the Korean Church for a century. It was from this revival that the Korean church began to be characterized by its zeal for prayer, Bible study and evangelism. It may be said that through this revival the Korean Church was born in a true sense.

Recently, however, Korean church historians have tended to understand the cause and effect of this Revival in a different way than the traditional one. Perhaps influenced by some Korean social scientists who interpret everything from a socio-political perspective, they argue that the revival was not a result of the work of the Holy Spirit but a mere product of missionaries who were aiming at the depoliticization of the Korean church.[23] That is to say, the missionaries wanted to call Korean Christians' attention away from political and nationalistic issues to the "purely spiritual" ones. They also argue that this revival, so much focused on the repentance of personal sin, made Korean Christians blind to social and national issues.[24]

This argument, however, seems to be based on some seriously misleading presuppositions. One of these presuppositions is that the conviction of and repentance from personal sin conflicts with the realization of social and structural evil. According to this assumption, the less a Christian is interested in his/her personal sin, the more he/she is likely to have interest in social issues, and vice versa. If this is the case, it becomes impossible for the realization of the personal sin and the awareness of social problems to coexist in one Christian. A Christian will be concerned either with personal sin and repentance or with social evil.

This results from a misunderstanding of the nature of sin. Whether personal sin or social sin, their essence is the same in that they are sin. Insofar as they are sin, Christians cannot but have concern about them and stand against them.[25] It should not be rashly argued, therefore, that as the Great Revival resulted in conviction of and repentance from personal sin, it deprived Korean Christians of a socio-political concern. The fact that those who attended the revival did not immediately begin a violent resistance to Japan cannot be a ground on which to conclude that the revival depoliticized and denationalized the Koreans Christians. Violent action is not the only way through which one's political concern is expressed. As Chungmin Suh indicates, it is very likely that the revival, by deepening the Korean Christians' conviction of the unrighteousness of Japanese invasion, contributed to the strengthening of their national consciousness.[26]

The second distorted view of the revival concerns its origin and cause. The scholars who think that the revival depoliticized the Korean Church also argue that the revival resulted from the intention of the missionaries who wanted to divest the Korean Church of its political color. It is very difficult, however, to see how such phenomena as the following can be brought about by mere human efforts. The preacher, reports a witness,

> reached only the word 'my Father' when a rush of power from without seemed to take hold of the meeting. The Europeans described its manifestation as terrifying. Nearly everybody present was seized with the most poignant sense of mental anguish; before each one his own sins seemed to be rising in condemnation of his life. Some were spring to their feet pleading for an opportunity to relieve their consciences by making their abasement known, others were silent, but rent with agony, clenching their fists and striking their heads against the ground in the struggle to resist the power that would force them to confess their misdeeds. From eight in the evening till five in the morning did this same go on....many of the Koreans spent the night awake; some in prayer, others in terrible spiritual conflict. Next day the missionaries hoped that the storm was over and that the comforting teaching of the Holy

> Word bind up the wounds of yester-night but again the same anguish, the same confession of sins; and so it went on for several days.[27]

Several witnesses including the missionaries have left similar reports about the beginning and the progress of the Great Revival.[28] If one insists, nevertheless, that such supernatural phenomena were a human projection, it would either be because of an extreme prejudice against or an ignorance of the religious experience.

The March First Movement

The Japanese colonial government ruled the Korean people by the bayonet. Not only the military personnel and the policemen, but even the teachers and the public officers wore the long swords while on their duty. The long sword was the symbol of the threat and oppression. After the occupation of Korea, Japan launched into the economic exploitation of Korea. Having explored all the territories of Korea, the colonial government confiscated almost half of the land of Koreans. Many of them, losing their land which was inherited from their ancestors, were reduced to the status of tenants. Moreover, the government suppressed the growth of Korean capital by requiring the permission of the government for the starting of a new company.[29] Permission was required even to build a new church. All the religious publications were censored. Worship services and religious meetings were subject to surveillance. Teaching the Bible in the Christian schools was outlawed, and the use of the Japanese language was enforced in all the classes. To go abroad for travel or study was forbidden, while tens of thousands of Koreans were forced by the government to move to Manchuria. The Koreans were deprived of the freedom of speech, meeting and association. Discriminatory treatment between Koreans and Japanese was to be found everywhere: employment, payment, promotion, opportunity for education and application of the laws.[30] It would have been strange if resistance had not occurred under such an oppressive and exploitative regime.

In addition, contemporary international politics seemed to be favorable for Koreans attempting their independence. In January 1918, that is, toward the end of the First World War, Woodrow Wilson pronounced fourteen points in his address to Congress. It was the fifth point of self-determination that excited Koreans with the expectation that they might be able to restore independence: " A free, open-minded, and absolutely impartial adjustment of all colonial claims, based upon a strict observance of the principles that, in determining all such questions of sovereignty, the interests of the populations concerned must have equal weight with the equitable claims of the government whose title is to be determined."[31] In fact, several small nations were restoring their independence at that time: Czechoslovakia, Yugoslavia, and Romania from Austria; Poland, Finland, Estonia, Lithuania, and Latvia from Russia.[32]

It was Koreans living in foreign countries who showed the swiftest response to this international trend. In February 8, 1919, Korean students in Tokyo declared the independence of Korea and expressed their determination to fight until they achieved their goal. After this, some Christian students, church leaders, and Chondogyo (a Korean religion) leaders, challenged by the action of the students in Tokyo, also agreed to declare the independence of Korea on March 1. Thirty-three national representatives signed the Declaration of Independence.

On March 1, 1919, thousands of Koreans gathered at Pagoda Park in Seoul and heard the Declaration of Independence read in the name of thirty three leaders of the nation. After that, they rushed out into the street and demonstrated their desire for independence from Japan. With the declaration and demonstration in Seoul as a start, Korean people living in all towns and villages throughout the country began to rise up and ask for independence. They read the Declaration sent from Seoul and marched in the street. The number of Koreans who participated in the nation-wide demonstrations amounted to two million, from two hundred and twelve out of the two hundred and eighteen Korean counties. It was literally a nation-wide movement and it went on for more than a year. There has never been such a widespread nationalistic movement in the history of Korea.[33]

As is often seen in mass demonstrations, some excited Koreans began violent action, setting fire to public buildings. Essentially, however, it was a pacifistic movement, for Koreans demonstrators did not have any weapons. Nevertheless, the Japanese government responded to this demonstration in a most brutal way. They killed more than 7,500 Koreans indiscriminately and arrested about 47,000.[34]

Christians played a vital role in this nationalistic movement. They took part in all the stages of preparation for the declaration at Pagoda Park. Out of the forty eight persons who played central roles in its preparation, twenty four were Christians. Out of thirty three who signed the Declaration of Independence, sixteen were Christians. It was Christian students who distributed the Declaration to the whole country, and invited people to Pagoda Park on D-day.[35] In almost all towns and villages, it was at the churches that Koreans gathered to read the Declaration as a start to the demonstration.[36] Such rapid spread of the movement throughout the country owed much to 200,000 Christians and their churches.[37]

The damage the Korean Church suffered during this movement demonstrates how actively Christians were involved in it. According to the report from the 8th General Assembly of the Korean Presbyterian Church in the fall of 1919, 3,804 Presbyterians were arrested during this movement, 134 of whom were ordained pastors or elders. This number amounts to thirteen percent of all the pastors and elders of the Presbyterian Church at that time. In addition, forty seven were killed, and 1,642 had been in prison. Twelve Presbyterian churches and eight schools were destroyed.[38] The situation of the Methodist Church was not much different. In their annual conference that year, it was reported that out of twenty eight pastors, fourteen were in prison.[39] According to the statistics of the military police at the end of that year, among 19,525 arrested Koreans, Christians numbered 3,426, which was 17.6 percent of the whole: Christians were the largest religious group of all those arrested.[40] Considering that the Christian population was about one percent of the whole population, this was a remarkably high rate.

Through the March First Movement Korean Christians proved themselves to be the group which had the strongest national consciousness. Christianity was a religion conducive to patriotism and national awareness.

Shintoism and Korean Church

Shintoism is a native Japanese religion which worshipped 'Kami.' A Japanese word, 'Kami' indicates a deity, or a spiritual being. From ancient times, Japanese worshipped as Kami awesome natural phenomena, mythological figures, historical heroes, and the spirit of their ancestors.[41] Shintoism, therefore, can be said to be a polytheistic religion handed down from a primitive age. In accordance with the absolutization of the power of emperors, the focus of Shinto began to move to the worship of the Sun goddess, the progenitress of the Japanese royal house.

The emperors naturally became the high priests of the Shinto worship. Shinto and the emperors were, therefore, indissolubly linked.[42]

Since antiquity, Buddhism had constituted the mainstream of Japanese religion. Since Shinto's doctrines and rituals were crude and primitive, it was in the position of a secondary religion. After the Meiji Restoration in 1868, however, Shinto began to emerge and take the position of the state religion. Meiji leaders attempted to make Shinto a foundation on which to build their imperial state. In 1882, Shinto was declared to be a "ritual of the state," not a "religion," and was separated from other religions. This measure was taken to ward off Western criticism that Japan violated such constitutional principles as the freedom of religion and separation of church and state. The true purpose of that measure, however, was to place Shinto over all the other religions.[43]

From the beginning of the twentieth century, the militaristic leaders of Japan began to use Shinto in their invasion of neighboring countries. Thus, the victories of Japan in the Sino-Japanese War in 1894 and in the Russo-Japanese War in 1904 were attributed to the Shinto. In the midst of the Manchurian Incident in 1931 and the Sino-Japanese War in 1937, the militaristic character of Shinto was more and more strengthened.

Enforcement of Shrine Worship in Korea

In 1918, Japan began to build a Shinto shrine in Seoul, and finished it in 1925. Until then, however, shrine worship was not enforced upon Koreans. It was in 1931, the year Japan invaded Manchuria, that the Japanese government began to force shrine worship upon Koreans. The chauvinistic militarists who prevailed in Japan in the 1930s required shrine worship of Koreans as an expression of the Koreans' unconditional loyalty to the Japanese emperor.[44]

The first target of the enforcement of the Shrine worship was the educational system. In 1932, the government imposed the obligation of shrine worship upon all the schools in Korea. However, the twenty-first General Assembly of the Presbyterian Church in Korea passed a resolution to refuse the shrine worship. In November 1935, the governor of Pyongnam Province called on a meeting of the principals of the middle schools, and at the opening of the meeting he directed them to worship at the shrine. G. S. McCune, V. L. Snook and H. M. Lee, the American missionaries who were serving as the principals in the Christian schools in

Pyengyang, refused to follow the direction. The governor warned them that if they continued to refuse the Shrine worship, a drastic measure would be taken. In December, however, the Northern Presbyterian Mission confirmed the policy of refusal of the Shrine worship notifying the governor of their stance. In January 1936, the governor revoked the authorization of McCune and Snook, and accordingly, McCune had to return to America. In February, Dr. Darby Fullton, the General Secretary of the Board of Foreign Mission in the Southern Presbyterian Church in America visited Korea. He was knowledgeable concerning Japan and Shinto, having been born and raised in Japan where his father had been president of the Kansai Theological Seminary. During his stay in Korea, Dr. Fullton made an announcement that shrine worship was an unquestionably religious action and that if the Japanese authorities continued its enforcement, all the schools under the supervision of the Southern Presbyterian Mission would close their doors. The Governor-General Minami, nevertheless, did not stop the demand that the Christian schools sponsor shrine worship, and all ten schools that belonged to the above denomination were closed.[45]

In the meantime, the Northern Presbyterian Mission had been investigating the meaning and the purpose of the Shrine worship. In March 1937, the result of the investigation was reported to all the missionaries by letter. The point of the report was that Shrine worship was a religious activity that was composed of praise of the gods and prayer for their blessings. According to this report, they closed eight middle schools under their Mission.[46]

In contrast to this, the Vatican declared to the Japanese Catholics in May 1932 that they might worship in the Shinto shrine, for Shrine worship was no more than a ritual that expressed patriotism and loyalty to the state. A note of the same purport was sent to the Korean Catholics in May 1936. This was exactly the opposite to what had been stipulated in the bylaws of the Korean Catholic Church: "The Catholics should not worship in the Shrine, for it is a place to worship other gods." The Methodist Church also did not have any problem with regard to the Shrine worship. They allowed their people to worship in the shrine accepting the statement of the government that Shinto worship was not a religious practice, but a duty for every citizen.[47]

Encouraged by the surrender of the Catholic and the Methodist Church, the government began to demand that the Presbyterian Church worship in the Shrine. In February 1938, the Pyongbuk Presbytery, the largest Korean presbytery, passed a resolution to worship in the Shrine. Until September of the same year, seventeen out of twenty-three presbyteries followed the precedent of the Pyongbuk presbytery. Finally, the General Assembly of 1938, which was held under the threat and operation of the Japanese police, surrendered to the pressure of the government and passed a resolution to worship at the Shrine. Thus, there remained no denomination in Korea which officially refused the Shrine worship.[48]

Not all Christians, however, submitted to the demand of the Shrine worship. In 1939, Elder Kwanjoon Park threw out copies of a petition to the Imperial parliament which was discussing the new laws on religion. In that petition, he asked the government to repeal the enforcement of the shrine worship. He was arrested and returned to Korea. After persistent efforts to oppose the shrine worship in Korea, he was imprisoned and died there. The famous martyr Rev. Gichul Joo was put into prison for seven years and died there in 1944. The congregation of Sanjunghyon Presbyterian Church which Rev. Joo served also consistently refused the shrine worship and was closed by the government. Rev. Sangdong Han and Giseon Yi attempted in vain to constitute presbyteries and a General Assembly which were composed of the Christians who refused the shrine worship. They were arrested, put to prison and saw the emancipation of their country while in prison. During the opposition movement to shrine worship, more than two thousand Korean Christians were imprisoned, fifty died, and more than two hundred churches were closed.[49]

Some denominations which emphasized the doctrine of the return of Christ were even ordered to dissolve themselves. In 1942, thirty-two pastors of the Korean Baptist Church were arrested, and the denomination was dissolved in 1944. Two hundred pastors of the Holiness Church also were arrested in May 1943, and a few months later the denomination was ordered to be dissolved. The Adventist Church went through the same fate in 1943.[50]

Those who refused to worship in the Shrine and chose to be persecuted did so not because of any political or nationalistic reason, but because of religious conviction. They simply did not want to defile their purity of faith by violating the first of the Ten Commandments. Nevertheless, it was taken by Japanese authorities as an action of serious political implication. They accepted it as a defiance of the foundation of their state, that is, the emperor system. For them, their emperor was equal to or higher than the Christian God. Accordingly, Korean Christians' refusal of shrine worship, which was closely related to the deification of the emperor, was a serious threat to the foundation of their state.[51] Even some Korean pastors' emphasis on the doctrine of Jesus' second coming was taken by Japanese as a threat to their state system, for the teaching that Jesus comes again to destroy all the earthly nations and establish his Kingdom was nothing but a direct contradiction to their belief that Japan was divine and eternal.[52] That was the reason why the Japanese government was so anxious to secure the surrender of Korean Christians with regard to shrine worship.

Traitorous Christians

After being engaged in a war with America, Japan began to demand more and more of the Korean Church. Not a few Korean church leaders, having surrendered to the demand of Shrine worship, had to yield to other endless demands of Japan. After 1938, we find them losing any hope of restoring their country. The articles that appear in *Tongyangzikwang* (meaning "The Light of Orient")— a magazine sponsored by the colonial government and published by Huido Park[53]— demonstrate how some of the Korean church leaders were corrupted at that time. Hungwoo Shin, the former General Secretary of YMCA, declared:

> To love Korea is to love Japan, and is possible only by becoming a faithful subject of Japanese Empire. We should not forget that we are Japanese before we are Christians, or Koreans....Love only Japan as a faithful legitimate sons of the emperor! Out of love of Japanese Empire, obey and cooperate with the policies of the Empire with all strength. This is the command of God given to our Korean Christians. I dare believe so.[54]

In 1939 the Korean Presbyterian Church formed the so-called "Mobilization of the Spiritual Power of the People," and, in the General Assembly of that year, was reporting that there had been 3,793 prayer meetings for the victory of Japan in the war. In 1940, the Korean Methodist Church decided to change herself into the wartime structure while the Presbyterian Church pronounced its shift to Japanese Christianity. The thirty-first General Assembly of the Presbyterian Church in 1942 announced a donation of money for fighter planes and machine guns and made the resolution to encourage Korean people to respond positively to conscription.[55] Taeyong Choi, a bishop in the Evangelical Church, proclaimed that God's will for Korean Christians was to pledge an absolute allegiance to Japan:

> It is God who handed over Korea to Japan. I think, therefore, that we should serve Japan as we serve God. Today we Koreans have only one state, that is, Japan....We are commanded by God to give our dearest to Japan, that is, to send our sons to the battlefield.[56]

Thus the Korean Church became a handmaiden to the militaristic state. The integrity of many church leaders was ruthlessly trampled down by the secular authorities.

Japan was not satisfied with this abject submission of the Korean Church to their demands. Despite the docile attitude of the church leaders, if the surrender of Japan in World War II had been delayed just a few days more, most Korean Christians would have been slaughtered. When America defeated Japan in the Philippines, Japan, afraid of the Korean Christians' cooperation with the American troops which, Japan thought, would soon arrive at Korea, planned to massacre all Korean Christians. The D-day for that action was August 18.[57] After the war, a cave in Youngbyon was identified by a Korean who had been an inspector under Japan as a place where Japan planned to kill 27,000 Korean Christians by using the Japanese sword and the bamboo spear.[58]

Conclusion

The first Korean Christians, although they were but a very small number, were characterized by their intense concern with and an active participation in the socio-political and nationalistic issues. The members of the Independent Club were typical of such Christians. Until the end of the nineteenth-century, at least, Christian faith contributed to an awakening of the Korean national consciousness.

From the beginning of the twentieth-century, there began to emerge a tendency in the Korean Church to make a complete separation between religion and politics. Such a task of depoliticizing the Korean Church was undertaken by the missionaries who did not want to promote a conflict with Japan. As their supreme purpose was to continue their missionary work in Korea regardless of Korea's national fate, or of the moral rightness of Japan's takeover of Korea, they found it wise not to involve themselves in sensitive issues between Korea and Japan. They justified their stand on the pretext of "separation of church and state." Many Korean Christians including most church leaders were persuaded by this theology of the missionaries on the relationship between religion and politics. From this time on, that is, from the first decade of the twentieth-century the Korean Church's tradition of political indifference began to be established.

Nevertheless, Korean Christians played a decisive role in the March First Movement of 1919, which was the greatest nationalistic movement in the history of Korea. Here the Korean Christians' desire for the independence of their nation overcame the missionaries' doctrine that Christians should devote themselves only to 'spiritual' or 'evangelical' matters.

For almost one decade around 1940, many of the Korean church leaders participated in a betrayal of their faith and their country by words and deeds. It was the darkest period in the Korean church history before the Emancipation.

As a whole, the history of the Korean Church in its relation to the state can be said to have been one of a "nationalistic" church. In spite of its weaknesses, it had been one of the most important factors in Korean society in strengthening the Korean people's national awareness and their political consciousness.

1 Mahn Yol Yi, *Korean Christianity and the National Consciousness* (Seoul: Gishik Sanubsa, 1991), 279.

2 *Taehan Christian Hwaebo*, No. 3-9 (March 1, 1899).

3 Yongha Shin, *Modern Korean History and the Problem of Nationhood* (Seoul: Munhakkwa Giseongsa, 1990), 111-2, 117.

4 Mahn Yol Yi, *National Consciousness*, 471.

5 John M. B. Sill's circular letter, "To Citizens of the United States present in Korea," May 11, 1897.

6 Andrew. J. Grajdanzev, *Modern Korea* (New York: John Day Co., 1944), 32.

7 In July 29, 1905, Taft, the American Secretary of the Army, sent by the President Theodore Roosevelt, exchanged a note with Katsra, the Prime Minister of Japan, the content of which was that America acknowledged the Japanese right of being a protectorate over Korea on the condition that Japan acquiesces in America's occupation of the Philippines. Tyler Dennet, "President Roosevelt's Secret Pact with Japan," *Current History*, Vol. 21, No. 1, Oct. 1924, 15-29.

8 John K. Fairbank, Edwin O. Reischauer, and Allen M. Craig, *A History of East Asian Civilization* Vol. II (Boston: Houghton Mifflin Co., 1965), 481.

9 The Institute of Korean Church History Studies, *A History of Korean Church* Vol. I (Seoul: The Christian Literature Press, 1990), 275.

10 *Ibid.*, 293-5.

11 *Ibid.*, 290.

12 *Ibid.*, 295-302.

13 *Taehan Maeil Shinbo* [Korea Daily News], March 25, 1908.

14 The Korea Information Papers, The Board of Foreign Missions of the Presbyterian Church in U. S. A., New York. These papers consist of reports and private letters on historical matters connected with the opening of mission stations in the interior, and on politico-missionary problems in Korea.

15 *Ibid.*

16 Report to the Quadrennial General Conference, the Journal of the 25th Delegated General Conference, Methodist Conference in 1908, 860.

17 The Government-General in Korea, *The Rule of Chosen and Christianity* (Seoul, 1921), 6.

18 L. George Paik, *The History of Protestant Missions in Korea: 1832-1910* (Seoul: Yonsei University Press, 1980), 414.

19 Letter of Rev. Wade Koons, Feb. 4, 1908 in Korean Information Papers.

20 W. N. Blair, *Gold in Korea* (Presbyterian Church in the U. S. A., 1957), 61-2.

21 In May 22, 1882, Korea and the United States made a treaty, the first article of which stipulated that if a third party treats one of the two treaty partners with injustice or violence, the other partner should immediately take a favorable action for the partner country.

22 Homer B. Hulbert, *The Passing of Korea* (New York: Doubleday, Page & Company, 1906), 223.

23 Kyongbae Min, *Church History of Korea* (Seoul: The Christian Literature Society of Korea, 1973), 213; Daejoon Rho, "The Nature of the Great Revival in 1907," in *Studies of History of Korean Christianity* No. 15-16 (August, 1987).

24 Mahn Yol Yi, *National Consciousness*, 250-253.

25 Why is it then, someone will ask, that some Christians who are sensitive to the matter of personal sin are not interested in the matter of social sin? In my judgment, it will be one of the two cases: 1) they have not had enough chance to learn about and recognize the existence of social evil, 2) they just pretend to be concerned exclusively with the matters of personal sin, while the true reason for their indifference to the social issues is their preference for the status quo. In the latter case, they are not really concerned about the personal sin, either.

26 Chungmin Suh, "Understanding the Great Revival of the Early Korean Church: With the Special Reference to Its Relation to the Nationalistic Movement," *Korean Christianity and the Nationalistic Movement*, edited by Mahn Yol Yi and other six writers (Seoul: Bosung Publishing Co., 1986), 275-280.

27 Lord Cecil, quoted by the *Baptist Missionary Magazine*, Vol. 88, No. 2 (Feb, 1908), 58.

28 For example, Rev. W. L. Swallen, "God's Work of Grace at Pyengyang Classes," *Korea Mission Field* Vol. III, No. 5, 78.

[29] During the World War I, there were arising 1,880 companies in Japan every year, but only one in Korea. Keun Ho Song, *Modern Korean History* (Seoul: Tureh Publishing co., 1986), 74-5.

[30] The Institute of Korean Church History Studies, *A History of Korean Church* Vol. II, 24-5.

[31] Leonard W. Doob, *Patriotism and Nationalism* (New Haven, Conn., Yale University Press, 1964), 211-212.

[32] Kibaek Yi, *A New History of Korea* (Seoul: Ilchogahk, 1990), 433-4.

[33] Jinbong Kim, "The March First Movement and the People," in *The Collection of Articles in Memory of the Fiftieth Anniversary of the March First Movement* (Seoul: Dong Ah Daily News, 1969), 351-61.

[34] Eunshik Park, *The Bloody History of Korean Independent Movement* (Seoul, Dahnkuhk University Press, 1975), 534-55.

[35] Mahn Yol Yi, *National Consciousness*, 347-8.

[36] The Institute of Korean Church History Studies, *A History of Korean Church*, Vol. II, 35-36 and footnote 26.

[37] Mahn Yol Yi, *National Consciousness*, 339.

[38] The Compilation Committee of the History of Independent Movement, *Collection of the Materials about the Independent Movement* Vol. 4, 476-7.

[39] Report of the twentieth Annual Conference of Korean Methodist Episcopal Church in 1919, p. 82.

[40] Mahn Yol Yi, *National Consciousness*, 349-350.

[41] Syngtae Kim, "The Invasion of the Japanese Shinto and the Problem of Shrine Worship in the 1920s and 1930s," *Korean Christianity and the Problem of Shrine Worship* ed. Syngtae Kim (Seoul: The Institute of Korean Church History Studies, 1991), 193ff.

[42] The objects of the Shinto worship these days are Sun Goddess, the mythological founder of Japan, that is, the alleged progenitress of the imperial house, all the emperors in the history of Japan, the royal family, subjects who distinguished themselves by their loyalty to the emperor or patriotism, and the progenitors of the clans. Jungmok Son, "A Study of the Policy of the Government-General in Korea to Spread the Shrine and Enforce the Shrine Worship," *Korean Christianity and the Problem of Shrine Worship*, 249-251,

[43] Syngtae Kim, "The Invasion of Shinto," 195-6.

[44] Yangseun Kim, "The Enforcement of the Shrine Worship and Persecution," *Korean Christianity and the Problem of the Shrine Worship,* 19-22.

[45] Sawa Masahiko, "The Problem of the Shrine Worship and the Christian Schools," *The Korean Christianity and the Problem of the Shrine Worship*, 393-427.

[46] Suk Hi Hahn, "The Enforcement of the Shrine Worship and Resistance to it," *The Korean Christianity and the Problem of the Shrine Worship*, 64-66.

[47] Yangseon Kim, "The Enforcement of the Shrine Worship," 28.

[48] *Ibid.*, 30-33.

[49] Yangseon Kim, 33-41; Suk Hi Hahn, 79-96.

[50] Kyung Bae Min, *Church History of Korea*, 351-3.

[51] Kurata Masahiko, *A History of the Japanese Persecution of Korean Church* (Seoul: The Christian Literature Press, 1991), 73, 67, 27, 16, 65.

[52] See the judgment of Rev. Yangwon Sohn by the Japanese judge in 1941. Syngtae Kim, *Korean Christianity and the Problem of the Shrine Worship*, 451-55.

[53] Huido Park was one of the thirty three signatories in the Declaration of Independence in 1919.

[54] Hungwoo Shin, "A Duty of Korean Christians for the Nation," *Tongyangzikwang* (Feb., 1939): 346.

[55] The Institute of Korean Church History Studies, *A History*, 310-18; Kyung Bae Min, *Church History of Korea*, 353-8.

[56] Taeyong Choi, "A New Start of the Korean Christian Church," *Tongyangzikwang* (Oct., 1942): 346.

[57] Blair, *Gold in Korea*, 111; S. H. Moffet, *The Christians of Korea*, 75-6.

[58] Jungchang Muhn, *A Korean History of Thirty Six Years under the Militaristic Japan* (Seoul: Paikmuhndang, 1066), 550.

CHAPTER V

CHURCH AND STATE IN KOREA (1945-PRESENT)

This chapter will discuss how the Reformed churches in Korea exercised their political responsibilities after Korea was emancipated from the occupation of Japan. It will particularly focus on how a representative conservative Presbyterian church, the *Habdong* denomination, responded to some decisive moments in Korean history. The *Habdong* church is not only the largest Presbyterian denomination in membership, but also has possessed, for a long time, channels for expressing its political views: a weekly newspaper *The Christian Times*,[1] and an academic journal *Shinhakjinam*.[2] Through the articles published in these periodicals, we can gain access to the political positions of this denomination.[3]

Christians and the First Republic of Korea

During the Japanese occupation, Koreans were almost entirely excluded from the political process. Political power was monopolized by the Japanese rulers. After August 15, 1945, when Korea was emancipated from Japan, the situation changed completely. With the sovereignty of the nation returned to Koreans, the chance for political participation was widely opened for all Koreans.

At the time of emancipation, Christians were the only group equipped with political experience. While most Koreans had been accustomed to political passivity under Japanese occupation for about four decades, Christians had opportunities for political training through church life. With a nationwide organization, they had lived out the beliefs and values which they learned in the Bible. In addition, the church was an institution operating on democratic principles.[4] It was natural, therefore, that Christians came to play a significant role in the establishment of the new Korean government.

Immediately after the emancipation, pastors and elders in northern Korea began to create political parties. In September 1945, pastors Kyung Jik Han and Ha Young Yoon organized the "Christian Socialist

Democratic Party." Two month later, elder Man Shik Cho and pastor Yoon Young Yi formed the "*Chosen* Democratic Party." In November, 1947, pastor Hwa Shik Kim organized the "Christian Liberal Party."[5] Although all these parties were forced by the Communists to dissolve, it is noteworthy that Christians, particularly the pastors, took the political initiative at the dawn of the new nation.

Among the national leaders who returned from exile, there were also significant numbers of Christians. Syng Mahn Rhee was one of them.[6] Partly owing to his career as a national leader for the independence of Korea, and partly because of his brilliant educational background, he was elected president of the first Republic of Korea.[7] The people's expectation of Christianity also contributed to his election. Having experienced that Buddhism and Confucianism, the state religions for thousands of years, did not work for the corporate salvation of the nation, Korean people were putting their hope in a new religion, namely, Christianity. They observed that most developed Western countries were Christian.[8] Thus, when the first National Assembly was convened in May 31, 1948, around fifty out of the two hundred representatives were professing Christians. At the opening session, the acting chairman Syng Man Rhee asked the ex-pastor Yoon Young Yi to pray to God.[9] It was notable that such a Christian ceremony was accepted by the congressmen without resistance in Korea, where other religions had dominated for thousands of years.

In the ceremony to celebrate both the establishment of the government of the Republic of Korea and the Presidential inauguration, Lee prayed for God's blessing.[10] Korean Christians were deeply impressed by the piety of their new president. Expecting him to play a role in the Christianization of Korea, they were determined to support him to the utmost of their capacity.[11]

Church's Support for the Christian Politicians

In August 1952, a few days prior to the election of the president and vice-president, the chairman of the Korean National Council of Churches summoned a meeting of the representatives of all denominations, including the Presbyterian Church, the Methodist Church, the Holiness Church and the Salvation Army. The purpose of the meeting was to organize a committee of the Korean churches for the presidential election and to decide who of five presidential candidates the churches would officially support in the election. Soon they reached a unanimous consensus to support Syng Mahn Rhee in the campaign and proclaimed their decision to all the churches in Korea. The stated reasons for their choice of Lee as president were simple: first, during his four year term, Lee changed the 'bowing' to the national flag into 'attention' to it. Second, he ordered that there should be chaplains in the military. Third, he directed that all national ceremonies be observed in a Christian manner.[12] These outward measures were enough to convince the church leaders that President Lee was a good Christian leader who had made a great contribution to the Christianization of Korea. During the campaign of 1952, *The Christian News* praised Lee as "a patriotic father of the nation," and "the great leader." To vote for Lee was a "duty entrusted to all Koreans who love their country."[13]

The Committee for the Election also decided to support an ex-pastor, Yoon Young Yi, in his vice-presidential campaign. The reason why Korean Christians were to vote for him was also simple: Yi attended worship services regularly and remembered his pastoral role even after entering the political world. His winning an election also would contribute to the "Christianization" of Korea.[14] To win the election, the Central Committee for Election in Seoul sent one committee member to every province entrusting them with a mission to organize a provincial committee and the local church committee for the election.[15]

No one raised the question as to whether or not the church could be lawfully mobilized for the election campaign giving official support to particular candidates. No discussion took place at that time of the issue of separation of church and state.

An Unjust Christian Government

Despite the significant number of Christian congressmen and Christians as the highest government officials, it was not long before Koreans sensed a conflict between the politicians' Christian profession and their practical politics. Korean Christians had been too naive in believing that all the professing Christians would represent their Christian values and beliefs in politics.

One of the first mistakes Syng Mahn Rhee made was that he promoted the collaborators with Japan to high positions in the government. In Korea at this time, this was not just against the nationalistic feeling of the people but it also violated the principle of justice. Collaboration was always regarded as the greatest sin in the eyes of the people who lost their country. Nevertheless, Syng Mahn Rhee appointed many collaborators to important posts. It was not without reason, of course, for him to have done so. Few Koreans had experience as professional high-ranking public officials at that time. Therefore, it was inevitable, to some extent, for President Lee to accept these experienced politicians. Above all, Lee needed them for the consolidation of his power.[16] The problem with this, however, was that while the collaborators were admitted to prestigious positions, the former patriots who fought for the independence of Korea during the Japanese occupation were not given adequate rewards. Thus, the first page of the history of the new Republic was stained by the record of unjust rewards.[17] Korean desire to purge the past and make a new start was thwarted. To many people, Syng Mahn Rhee seemed more concerned with his own power than for the healthy development of the new Republic.

Toward the end of his second term, Rhee wanted to continue to hold on to his power. It was impossible, however, for him to do so lawfully, because there was an article in the Korean constitution that stipulated that one person could not be elected President more than twice. The only way for him to achieve his goal was to amend the constitution. So he had his party propose to the National Assembly that the first president of Korea should be the exception to the rule of limited term. According to the constitution, the amendment of the constitution required the approval of two-thirds of the Congress. At that time, there were 203 congressmen in Korea. Technically, the required number was 135.3333. Legally this meant that 136 affirmative votes were needed for the amending of the constitution. The result of the voting was 135 affirmative and 60 negative; so the proposal was announced to have been rejected. After two days, however, Syng Man Rhee's party revoked their previous assessment and announced that the proposal had been passed by rounding out to the nearest whole number. Through this questionable move, Lee extended his term. Strictly speaking, however, Syng Man Rhee can be said to have lost his moral legitimacy after his second term.

The Korean Church was not mature enough to be sensitive to such a serious injustice. It did not cease to give blind support to Syng Mahn Rhee and the so-called Christian politicians. In the 1954 general election, the Christian newspaper engaged in the campaign by introducing the Christian candidates' profiles.[18] In the third presidential election, *The Christian News* praised Syng Mahn Rhee as a "Korean Moses."[19]

In the third presidential election in 1956, however, some reflections emerged on the nature of the churches' role in politics. *The Christian Press* warned the churches of the candidates' attempt to use them for their election. Since the church is not a "political agency," it argued, it should not collectively support a particular candidate in the name of the church, nor should it be engaged in the campaign. This was a flat contradiction to the previous practice of the churches. While the newspaper did not express any repentance regarding its active involvement in the past campaigns, it did call upon the churches to play a prophetic role. The church, it said, should be able to "criticize the injustice of the state."[20] Perhaps influenced by this mood, when the Christian Committee for the Presidential Election was organized on April 11, the Committee made it clear that it did not represent the denominations or Christian organizations but was acting on behalf of individual citizens.[21]

April Revolution and the Church

It is widely recognized that power corrupts and that absolute power corrupts absolutely. As the reign of one leader was extended, a tendency toward corruption emerged in the Korean government, even among Christian politicians. Some Christian congressmen caused a scandal by being involved in smuggling.[22] One government officer, who had been a pastor, was reported to have taken the initiative in shutting down a nation-wide daily newspaper because of its critical position toward the government.[23]

In the presidential election on March 15, 1960, Syng Man Rhee's party and his government utilized corrupt election practices for Rhee and his running mate, Ki Boong Lee, another professing Christian. When college students, and even high school students, along with other citizens angrily demonstrated in the streets the government ordered the police to fire on them. One hundred and eighty seven students were killed and more than five thousand were wounded. Nevertheless, the protests got more and more vehement. Finally, on April 19, 1960, President Rhee announced that he would resign his presidency. This was the end of what was called the 'Christian government.'

The church's attitude toward Lee's regime changed drastically overnight. Before the April Revolution, the church had said nothing critical about the corruption and misrule of Lee's government. Rather, it had regularly expressed its support for the government. But when Lee's government was overthrown by the protest of the students, the church suddenly became very critical of it. On April 23, the United Association of Korean Churches issued a statement on the April Revolution. Comparing it favorably to the March First Movement of 1919, it called on the government to reform: guarantee of fundamental human rights; a purge of the government, the military and the police; establishment of democracy and rule by law; and the abolition of torture, etc.[24]

The Christian newspapers, which had kept silent during his term of office, also suddenly became very critical after the April Revolution. "We felt," *The Christian News* said, "that President Lee made so many mistakes" during his terms. It had been difficult to discern whether he was an "emperor" or a "president." He ruled for the sake of himself rather than for the sake of the people. "During his twelve year term, the government got more and more corrupt." "Most Protestant politicians brought disgrace rather than honor upon the church."[25]

Since the church had always been in a close relationship with Rhee's government, most Christians were shocked to see that the dictatorial government was overthrown overnight.[26] One scholar has argued that the church should have issued a statement of repentance after the Revolution, because it had blindly cooperated with such an unjust regime.[27] The churches, however, did not go through a period of serious reflection after the Revolution. Instead, they experienced a serious conflict in their own internal affairs. By that time, the Korean Presbyterian Church, the largest Christian denomination of Korea, was going through a division on the issue of its relationship with World Council of Churches. Indeed, after the military coup broke out, the Korean churches were warned by General Park, the coup leader, that if they continued to fight among themselves, the government would deprive them of the right to worship.[28]

The Second Republic

At the cost of thousands of student lives, the corrupt and dictatorial regime of Syng Mahn Rhee was overthrown, and after the amendment of the constitution on June 15, the second Republic was established on August 2, 1960. The new government was now given a parliamentary form. This meant that while a Presbyterian Bosun Yoon was elected president,[29] the actual power was in the hand of the prime minister Myon Chang, a Roman Catholic.

It was not long, however, before Chang's government came to be plagued by inefficiency. Unlike Lee's dictatorial government, this regime was too weak and irresolute. It failed to provide sufficient leadership to a society in confusion after the revolution. Daily demonstrations occurred in which crowds of people insisted on their own rights. Soon the same corrupt politicians who worked under Lee returned to their positions and repeated the same policies for the sake of their own interests. Even though a democratic government was apparently established, nothing substantial seemed to have been changed. Poverty and disorder prevailed in the society. Conditions were ripe for a military takeover.

On May 16, 1961, less than a year after the launching of the Second Republic, some politically ambitious military officers under the leadership of General Chung Hee Park carried out a successful coup. Park was aware that the government had been planning to force him to retire at the end of May.[30]

Church and 5. 16

Many ordinary people welcomed the coup, because under the iron-fisted rule of the military leadership the order of society was rapidly restored. This was what they had been seeking since the April Revolution. The church also responded favorably to the military regime. Just ten days after the coup, the Korean National Council of Churches (hereafter, KNCC) issued a statement justifying and praising the military intervention. The coup, it said, was "inevitable" to save the country from the "invasion of the Communists" as well as from "injustices and corruption." Therefore, it argued, the Korean people had to be supportive to the military government.[31]

The Christian News seemed anxious to flatter the military leaders. When the coup broke out, the paper said, the commander of the army of the United Nations and the American Ambassador in Korea opposed it, because they thought that Chang's government was the only legitimate one in Korea. But if the coup leaders had surrendered to their pressure, it continued, "Korea would have degenerated into one of the American colonies." "The united power of Koreans beat the United States....The military coup proved the independence of Korea, which had been long misunderstood as a puppet of the United States." *The Christian News* mentioned nothing about the negative dimensions of the military coup: the encroachments on democracy, freedom and human rights. "We are happy now to be under the authoritative government," it said. "We want to see the unbridled restrained even at the cost of our freedom."[32]

Three months after the coup, General Park promised the people that the coup leaders would hand the reins over to civilian rule. In March 16, 1963, however, he suggested a proposal to prolong the military rule four more years and to put the proposal to a national plebiscite. At this, Korean National Council of Churches issued a statement to call upon General Park to keep his previous promise to turn the government over to the civilians and return to the military. "The proclamation of the person in the most responsible position of a country," said the statement, "affects the dignity of the country."[33] This was the first significant political role played by the Korean churches although the conservative denominations were not members of the Council.

The American President John F. Kennedy also strongly opposed the prolongation of the military government in Korea. He threatened to stop America's economic support for Korea.[34] Finally, on April 8, Park announced that he would withdraw his proposal. He retired in August, ran for election to the presidency and won the election. After two and half years of military rule, he was inaugurated as president on December 17, 1963.

Normalization of Diplomatic Relationship with Japan

The first confrontation of the church and Park's government occurred in 1965 on the issue of normalization of diplomatic relations between Korea and Japan. Park's government was anxious to restore the relationship with Japan in order to develop the Korean economy by drawing on Japanese money. In the ordinary Koreans' eyes, however, the government was hurrying the process. In addition, they felt, the government was making an unfair and humiliating concession.[35] The Korean people's nationalistic feeling could not accept this normalization. The opposition movement to "normalization" began in the colleges and spread throughout the country. On July 1, 1965, more than two hundred church leaders, including Kyung Jik Han, Jae Joon Kim, Won Yong Kang and Suk Hun Ham, issued a statement opposing the 'normalization.'[36] Now even the conservative churches spoke out. On July 3, the officers of *Habdong* Denomination, the largest of the conservative Presbyterian denominations in Korea, met at Syngdong Church and decided to proclaim the week beginning on July 4 as a week of prayer. During this week all the local churches in that denomination were supposed to pray for the nation in crisis. They also decided that for three days, from July 8 to 10, each presbyter in that denomination should hold a fast-and-prayer meeting for the country.[37] On July 8, during the pray-and-fasting meeting for pastors at Pyong Ahn Church in Seoul, the assembled clergy including the leaders of the *Habdong* denomination sent a petition to the government expressing their objection to the "normalization."[38] This seems to be the first and the last occasion in which the Habdong denomination acted to express objections to the government regarding a political issue.

In the middle of the sixties, the *Habdong* denomination did not have a strongly negative attitude toward Christian social responsibility. On June 21, 1965, the editorial of the denominational newspaper, *The Christian Times*, dealt with the topic of social concern. Introducing the new Confession of Faith of the Presbyterian Church of USA, it noted that one of the major features of the Confession was an emphasis on the Christian social responsibility. Surprisingly, it responded in this positive way:

> We cannot emphasize the importance of the Christian social involvement too much in the sense that we should not stop at securing the individual salvation but should proceed to be the light and salt of the world. Isn't it the reality of today that the Christians and their Church exert so little influence on the society that they have degraded into an object of derision?

The editorial went on to observe that if this inaction could be corrected by an article on Christian social responsibility in the Korean Presbyterians' own Confession of Faith, "we should not hesitate to revise our Confession and insert an article on that."[39]

This editorial, remarkable as it was, had its limits. By the term 'social influence,' it chiefly meant the personal influence of individual Christians on their neighbors: Society changes, the paper argued, "when each Christian believes and lives according to God's Word, for the Bible contains all the answers to the human and social problems." It did not mention structural evil, nor did it specify political options for Christians to remedy the political situation.

Until 1969, when President Park was making every attempt to amend the constitution to make his third term possible, the Habdong denomination maintained a careful balance on the relationship and responsibility of the church to the state. In the editorial of April 19, it criticized the "deep-rooted prejudice" that God's rule is confined to the "spiritual" matters and that only those are pious who ignore the "secular" matters. Furthermore, it maintained a position on the issue of political authority that echoed a Reformed tradition. "Whether it is to the spiritual authority or to the secular authority," it declared, "the saint's obedience to the authority should be rendered as far as the authorities perform their God-given duty faithfully, for the saint's obedience to the authority should be led by his/her obedience to God." As a conclusion, it called on the church to "wake up the rulers by bringing to light all the social evil." "Do not pretend to be spiritual," it cried, "acquiescing in the tyranny of the ruler in fear of death." On the other hand, *The Christian Times* showed a respectable balance by reproving the irresponsibility of those who attacked the rulers "without praying for them."[40]

Park's Amendment of the Constitution for the Third Term

It has proved to be true in Korea that power is something of an opiate. Toward the end of his second term, Chung Hee Park and his aides began plotting to prolong his reign. The obstacle to achieving this goal was the article in the Constitution which prohibited one person from running for the third presidential term. From the beginning of 1969, they set out to create an atmosphere for the amendment of the constitution. On July 25, 1969, at last, Park announced he would put the proposal of the amendment of the constitution to a national plebiscite. He warned that if the proposal were rejected in the plebiscite, he would accept it as evidence that Korean people distrusted him and would immediately resign from the presidential office. This tactic was designed to take advantage of the people's fear of the anarchy which would result from the vacuum of power.[41]

Many thinking Koreans opposed the amendment, fearing that the prolongation of one man's reign would inevitably result in the corruption of power. "A Committee to Oppose the Amendment of the Constitution for the Third Presidential Term" was organized by some dissident intellectuals and politicians, among whom were several church leaders of the liberal camp, such as Jae Joon Kim, Suk Hun Ham and Hyong Kyu Park. On August 15, this committee published a statement in the major daily newspapers to express their opposition to the amendment. In this statement, they stressed that the church should play the prophetic role by attacking unrighteousness and by committing itself to the cause of justice.[42]

On September 2, a week after that statement was issued, 242 pastors of the conservative churches made a counter-statement with the title of "The Amendment of the Constitution and the Proclamation of the Freedom of the Conscience." In this statement they accused the Jae Joon Kim's statement of "confusing the conscience of numerous simple laymen and laywomen." They insisted that the church should remain 'neutral' in political matters according to the principle of separation of church and state.[43]

Political "neutralism," of course is, a thinly disguised rationale for actively supporting the political status quo. Three days after the statement by 242 pastors was issued, another statement was issued by the Association of Conservative Churches, among whose members included the most eminent leaders of the conservative churches in Korea, such as Hyong Yong Park, Yoon Sun Park, Yong Gi Cho, Joon Gon Kim, Jang Hwan Kim and Yoon Chan Kim. These six men were among the 242 who had signed the "neutralist" declaration three days before. In this new declaration under the title of "Our Position on the Amendment of the Constitution", they acknowledged that "We Christians welcome the decision of President Park on the issue of the Amendment," and "want to see strong leadership in this kind of national and international situation."[44] Thus they did not remain neutral. They demonstrated that they could be as political as the liberals. As Jong Go Choi has argued, the real difference between the conservatives and the liberals was that the former were supportive of the government while the latter were critical of it.[45]

On September 6, the Korean National Council of Churches pronounced that it had nothing to do with the Association of the Conservative Churches; two days later it issued a statement to express its own "deep regrets and concerns" about the proposed Amendment.[46]

The Christian Times did not take exactly the same stance in this matter as the leading theologians of its denomination. In an editorial on the topic of church and state, it declared that the church and state should have some "interaction" with each other as long as the independence of each was not jeopardized. Therefore, it said, "the church should be able to give advice and suggestions to the rulers out of good motives." Since it also argued, however, that the separation of church and state meant that "political action" should not be taken in the name of the church and Christ, it was not clear what it actually meant by "political action." It went on to lament that the principle of separation of church and state was completely trampled down by senseless Christians and politicians. "The rulers," it stated, "were giving pressure to the church out of their political purposes"; politicians, even Christian politicians, were trying to "make use of the church" for their purposes; "the churches were flattering and making compromises with the political authorities in order to secure some interests."[47]

On October 17, the proposal for the Amendment was passed by a vote of 65% to 31%. In the next Presidential campaign of 1971, Park, who was running for the third term, promised the people that "This will be the last time for me to ask for your votes. For four years, I will eradicate corruption, preparing my successor."[48] Korean people accepted this as a promise that he would not seek to run again for the presidential office after his third term.[49]

Yushin Constitution

Chung Hee Park was not content, however, to let go of the power he enjoyed so much, even after a third term. Immediately after winning the election of April through various questionable means, Park secretly ordered some scholars to formulate a constitutional system which enabled him to hold the power as long as he wished. Suddenly, on October 17, 1971, through a special presidential proclamation, Park suspended some articles of the constitution, dissolved the National Assembly and banned political activities and party politics . At the same time, emergency martial law was also declared. Meetings and demonstrations for the political purposes were prohibited from that day forward, the press was required to submit to pre-censorship, and the colleges were temporarily closed.

After ten days, a proposal for the amendment of the constitution was publicly announced by the emergency state council. The purpose of the proposed constitution was to provide legal support for the perpetuation and absolutization of the power of one man, Chung Hee Park. According to this constitutional proposal, later to be called the Yushin Constitution, the president was to have almost total power: he had the right of dissolving the National Assembly as well as the right to nominate one-third of its total members; the term of the presidential office was extended from four to six years, and, most importantly, one could be repeatedly and limitlessly elected president. The president was also to have the power to appoint the Chief Justice with the approval of the National Assembly. He/she also had the right to propose amendments to the constitution as well as the right to take emergency measures by which the freedom and rights of the people could be suspended. Indeed, according to this new constitution, the president had rights equivalent to kings under a monarchy.

Another institutional device to secure Park's victory in the presidential election was included in the Yushin Constitution: "The National Council for the Promotion of Unification." Park stated that this institution was to seek ways for the reunification of South and North Korea. It was to be composed of 2,359 members who were chosen through the popular election in 1,630 electoral districts. In reality, however, it was intended to be a "rubber stamp" to elect the presidential candidate presented by the ruling party. Having won the 1971 presidential election by a narrow margin, Park seemed to have lost confidence in the standing system to elect the president through a direct popular election. So he decided to achieve his goal by changing the method of electing a president to an indirect election. 'The National Council for the Promotion of Unification' would perform that role. Here Park took clear advantage of the Korean people's desire for re-unification. He meant to guarantee his life-long reign by linking his power to the reunification of Korea. This was why, he argued, an amended constitution was a necessity.

Even though the Yushin constitution would inevitably lead to the destruction of democracy in Korea, Park's government argued that it was actually indispensable for the establishment of "Korean democracy." The national referendum for the adoption of the Yushin Constitution was announced to be held November 21, 1971. Although the college students, the intellectuals, the politicians of the opposite party, and some Christians felt this to be an unjust and tyrannical development, they could not express their opposition to the Yushin constitution because the emergency martial law prohibited any political activities.

At this time, *The Christian Times* began to feature a column under the title of "The Necessity of the 'Yushin' Constitution." Beginning from November 4, this column continued to appear in that paper for three consecutive weeks until three days before the referendum. The column almost literally echoed the logic and even the language used by the government in defending the Yushin constitution. The column began by stressing the necessity of "Korean democracy." "During the last thirty years," it argued, "we have used the democracy which we have borrowed from the Western countries." "Now," it continued, "it has become obvious that the unfamiliar Western democracy does not fit for our situation." Therefore, "we have come to prepare our own democracy which has been modified to suit our need."

The column went on to suggest that the people should be united in supporting and carrying out "this historical task" of Yushin for the following reasons. First, it was necessary for the reunification of Korea. "Now that the channel of South-North dialogue has been installed, we should support it through the change of the constitution."[50] It celebrated the fact that the Yushin Constitution included the article on The National Council for Reunification.[51]

The second reason suggested by the *Christian Times* for the necessity of the Yushin Constitution did not follow easily from the first argument. While the first rationale looked to reunification in the near future, the second presupposed the continuation of the cold war. "The state of division," it said, requires the Yushin constitution. "We have a fundamental difference from other countries....It is that we are divided into South and North....We should defend our country along 155 miles of truce line." Because of this special need of national defence, it argued, Koreans should not "make a fuss about such trifles" as democracy, human rights, and freedom. To do so is "against the prosperity of the nation." Just as America has American democracy and England its own English democracy, so "Korea should have Korean democracy....To adopt the Yushin constitution is to throw away the clothes we borrowed from others and wear the clothes of our own." This was very similar to the logic used by the government.[52]

The third rationale suggested by *The Christian Times* in support of the Yushin constitution was the reliability and infallibility of President Park. "Is there anything that has proved wrong that President Park planned and carried out?" the column challenged. "How miserable our situation would be now," it asked, "if he had not propelled, with all the criticisms and complaints, the plans for the economic development, the normalization of diplomatic relationship between Korea and Japan, and the construction of highways?" The "ordinary people" cannot easily understand what a "good leader" does, because he always acts "foreseeing the future." The Yushin Constitution, it argued, was one of these cases.[53]

The Yushin period was the time when the support of *The Christian Times* for the government reached its climax. Immediately before the 1973 general election, it carried another series under the title "The Cornerstone of the Korean Democracy." In these articles, it attacked the parliamentary institutions and party politics. "As President Park said," it stated, "looking back at the political history of the last quarter century, it was the inefficiency and the unproductivity of the parliament more than anything else that obstructed the maximization of the national power....This, in turn, was caused by the parties and the senseless politicians." Because of this "unreasonable political ethos of politics of our country," it argued, President Park, at Yushin, dissolved the parliament and suspended the political activities.[54] Thus the *Christian Times* attempted to argue that for the sake of the efficiency of the parliament Christians should support the ruling party of Chung Hee Park.

Professors at Chongshin Seminary

While *The Christian Times* was writing such articles in support of the dictatorial government, Ui Hwan Kim, a professor of Chongshin Seminary, wrote an article on "The Problem of the Political Involvement of the Korean Church" in the journal published by his seminary.[55] This article is noteworthy because it was the first piece written by a professor of Chongshin Seminary on the topic of church and state.

Kim argued that church and state must be separated completely since those two institutions have "a different purpose and function from each other." The church, he stressed, should not be involved "in the name of the church" in the non-religious matters. Individual Christians could be engaged in political actions, but the Church ought not to be "directly" involved in "political" reality.[56]

As examples of the church's "direct" involvement in political matters, Kim indicated Korean Christians' political actions at the end of the nineteenth-century, the Korean church's active involvement in the March

First Movement in 1919, its expression of objection to the "normalization" of the diplomatic relationship between Korea and Japan in 1965, and the debate on the Yushin constitution. He particularly stressed that Korean Church's active involvement in the March First Movement was a serious mistake for several reasons: first, because of its involvement in the nationalistic movement, the Korean Church was severely persecuted by the Japanese rulers; second, the Korean church leaders at that time failed to accept that the Japanese authorities were from God; third, Christianity had nothing to do with nationalism.[57]

Living in a country where democracy was constitutionally adopted, Kim did not show a strong belief in democracy. "Christians should not stick to the democratic form of government," he declared, "they should obey the authorities above whether they are the Roman government or something like that."[58] This was equivalent to saying that the Korean Christians should not be involved in the opposition movement to the dictatorial Park regime. The only occasion that the church could "speak out or protest against the state in the name of the church," he argued, was when the state "encroached upon the domain of the church, violating the chief doctrines of the Bible." Only with regard to "religious" matters in the narrower sense of the word, could the church speak to the government. All the other political actions by the church are mistaken; they "confuse Caesar's reign with God's."[59] In effect, Kim was advocating an apolitical attitude for the church.

In December 1973, a dissident group that was comprised of the politicians of the opposition party, professors, and liberal church leaders started a petition to collect one million signatures to amend the Yushin constitution. In order to block this movement, President Park announced the Emergency Measures I and II, on January 8, 1974. According to these extreme measures, 1) any action that "rejects, objects, or criticizes" the 'Yushin' constitution was outlawed; 2) whatever action that "maintains, suggests, proposes or petitions the amendment or abolition" of the 'Yushin' constitution was outlawed; 3) whoever "violates or criticizes" these measures shall be "arrested, searched, and confiscated without an arrest warrant and shall be sentenced to fifteen years' imprisonment"; 4) whoever violates or criticizes this measure shall be judged and condemned by the emergency court-martial.

In Fall of 1974 when the implications of 'Yushin' were being realized, Bong Ho Son, an adjunct professor at Chongshin Seminary, published two articles on social ethics in *Shinhak Jinam*. Son was a Christian philosopher from the 'Koshin' denomination, one of the most conservative Presbyterian denominations in Korea. In the article "The Problem of the Christian Social Ethics," he was dealing with the problem of 'structural evil,' or 'social evil.' "Institutions or structures," he stated, "have much greater and formidable power than individuals can have." Therefore, "bad institutions can result in inequity, injustice and evil no matter how good the individuals may be."[60] If Christians want to obey the greatest commandment, "Love your neighbor as yourselves," and if they do not want to "participate in this social structural evil," he continued, they must not only "be aware of this power of the institutions" but also "commit themselves to the task of social reform."[61] As a conclusion, he declared that the indifference of many evangelicals to social evil could not be excused under any pretext.[62]

This article stopped, however, at introducing the principles and necessity of social ethics. Perhaps because of the limitation of space, Son did not proceed to apply those principles to the real situation of Korea which was presently struggling with many serious issues related to social ethics.

In the next issue of *Shinhak Jinam*, Son published another article on the topic of social justice. This time, he discussed it in relation to Christian mission. Now his tone became more emphatic than in the previous article. They are "not worthy of the name 'Christians,'" he declared, "who keep silence in the sight of the oppression of the poor and the sick." Few Koreans would have asserted the prophetic role of the Christians as strongly as Son at that time:

> [Christians] ought to criticize and try to reform the unrighteousness of any government or any party. All the governments on the earth have a strong tendency to become unjust. That is the reason the Church and the missionaries, as idealists, cannot but be critical of them. That was the reason why the Old Testament prophets were always critical.[63]

As early as 1974, Son already had a very comprehensive understanding of "mission." Mission, for him, was not a mere verbal presentation of the gospel message. It required activities "as holistic as life itself, and these holistic activities included the realization of social justice." Therefore, for him, any mission which "avoided this dimension of social justice" was not genuine Christian mission. It was "a lame mission which ignores God's sovereignty and righteousness."[64]

In his effort to stress this comprehensiveness of gospel salvation, he introduced the term "liberation," which was still regarded as taboo for conservatives in Korea. "The Gospel of Jesus," he declared, "means the 'liberation' of the weak, the poor and the miserable." Therefore, he continued, "when the gospel is preached, such liberation should take place." Mere preaching the name of Christ could not bring about such liberation. In order for it to take place, the "social structure must be changed." God's way of realizing his justice also, Son asserted, was "standing on the side of the poor, the oppressed and the despised, and judging the oppressors."[65]

For Son, social justice was so vital an element in Christianity that he even argued that in order for a country to be qualified for overseas mission, a reasonable degree of social justice had to be realized in that country. The country of the missionary should be more just than the country to be evangelized. If not, "that country is yet premature as a missionary-sending country." Therefore, he concluded, "before we set out to the mission field, we should think over how much our church has contributed to the realization of justice in our society, and how much our society is just."[66]

Although these two articles by Bong Ho Son were no less sharp than any liberal theologian's writings in stressing the importance of social justice as an essential element of the gospel, these were far from expressing the general trend of the conservative churches in Korea. Most conservative Korean church leaders at that time would rather have followed the line of Ui Hwan Kim than that of Son in dealing with the issue of church and state.

Debate on Church and State

In the Fall of 1974, some of the highest government officials were complaining of the liberal church leaders' political involvement. On November 9, Prime Minister Jong Pil Kim made a speech at the breakfast prayer meeting for Christian businessmen. He complained that some pastors and Christians, forgetting their "original duty of preaching the gospel," were "inappropriately" engaging themselves in political actions through demonstration or instigation. This, he argued, was against the constitution that prohibited a religious institution's interference in politics "in any form." Kim warned that if they continued to "challenge the authority of the government" through preaching or demonstration, it would be inevitable that the government would punish them.[67]

As a rebuttal to Kim's speech, the KNCC issued a statement on the 18th of the same month. The teaching of Romans 13 that all powers are from God, it argued, "presupposed the legitimacy and limit" of political power. The government was "entrusted with a conditional authority by God" for the welfare of the people and for the order, peace and justice of the society. Therefore, when human authority goes beyond its limit and becomes unfaithful to its responsibility, the church, as the "trustee of the Word of God," is required to "criticize and correct" it. Furthermore, it continued, when governments stand against the will of God and attempt to perpetuate their power, the church ought to "refuse to cooperate with such governments and rather ought to withstand it."[68]

It was the association of the conservative churches, not the government, that responded promptly to this statement of the KNCC. In November 25, 1974, the conservative Korean Council of Christian Churches issued a statement saying that those who were critical of the government were causing "social disorder." Moreover, they argued, it was "unbiblical" for the Christians to issue anti-governmental statements and to participate in critical demonstrations. According to their standard of biblical attitudes regarding church-state relations, the church should pray for and obey the government as long as the government did not violate freedom of religion.[69]

On November 27, the Association of the Conservative Churches also issued a statement, arguing that the commandment of Romans 13 was "unconditional." "Think of how Paul acted under the Roman government," it said. "Such anti-governmental action as demonstration was only benefiting the Communist enemy" in North Korea. The statement ended with the insistence that the church should be devoted only to "saving souls through evangelism."[70]

A Pro-governmental Church Paper

While the conservative churches in Korea were actively making pro-government statements, *The Christian Times* argued in its column of November 30, 1974, that it was for the sake of "national security" that the conservative churches in Korea kept silent on the political situation.[71] In a second column under the same title, the *Times* attempted to support its own position by citing such New Testament passages as "Give to Caesar what is Caesar's, and to God what is God's" (Matthew 22:21) and "all who draw the sword will die by the sword" (Matthew 26:52). It did not provide, however, any detailed exegesis of those passages. It also argued that the duty of true Christians was to love their enemies and pray for their persecutors. By this it seemed to be implying that the contemporary Korean rulers had acted in such a way as to deserve to be called "enemies" or "persecutors" of Christians.[72] The column ended with the conclusion that the church should keep its distance from politics, because once the church gets involved in such "secular" affairs, it is very likely to degenerate.

Even after placing such a strong emphasis on the necessity of the church to keep away from political topics, *The Christian Times* itself never failed to write articles in support of the government when there emerged important political issues in Korea. On January 22, 1975, President Park announced that he would hold a referendum on February 12 to discern whether the people really supported the Yushin constitution and his regime. The dissidents rejected this plan, however, on the ground that the referendum that was held under such an oppressive atmosphere was a mere political "show." In order for a fair referendum to be held, they argued, the freedom of press and a free debate on the Yushin constitution should be first allowed.[73] The true intention of the government's proposal of the referendum, they believed, was to quiet the dissidents' demand for democratization by instituting an apparently lawful procedure.

At this time, *The Christian Times* again wrote an article overtly supporting Park's proposal for the referendum. After giving a lengthy explanation of the historical inevitability of the Yushin constitution, it advised: "Make a wise choice between prosperity and poverty,"[74] clearly implying voting for the referendum was choosing for prosperity.

Two weeks later, *The Christian Times* carried another article criticizing the demonstrations of the college students. Without making any mention as to why the students had come to be engaged in such political actions, the *Times* contended that it was wrong for the students, who would be in charge of the "tomorrow" of the country, to try to take part in "today's" issues. It insisted that "It is not the rulers or political leaders but the parents of the students that are to be accountable for all the irrationalities and injustices" of the country.[75]

In its editorial of April 26, 1975, *The Christian Times* expressed its strong inclination toward the status quo, expressing fear about the movement for the democratization of the country. The movements for democracy and social justice by students, Christians and the journalists, it stated, caused "unrest" rather than the "sympathy" of our people. It also endorsed the government's announcement that the communists' were at work in the students' attempt to demonstrate in April 1974 against the government.[76]

The End of Yushin and the Church

Despite all these attempted vindications of Park's government by *The Christian Times*, the discontent of the Korean people with Park's regime increased more and more, and finally on October 26 1979, Park was assassinated by a member of his government, Jae Kyu Kim, the chief of the Central Intelligence Agency of Korea. After several months of power struggle among the military leaders, General Doo Hwan Chun came to power in 1980. Chun also was one of Park's close followers.

The character of the Fifth Republic of Korea of Doo Hwan Chun was exactly the same as the authoritarianism of the Third and Fourth Republic of Chung Hee Park. Accordingly, the attitude of the conservative churches to the government in the eighties was basically the same as it had been in the seventies.

But the resistance of Korean people to the corruption and dictatorial rule of Chun increased more and more. Finally their demand for democratization reached its climax on June 29, 1987. Several months later, Chun retired and his regime was replaced by a more or less democratic government of Tae Uh Roh. Although Roh was also one of Chun's closest friends, he was also the first President since 1971 to be chosen through a direct popular election. Since his election, the entire Korean society has become more democratic. In order for these positive changes to take place, the efforts and sacrifices of the dissidents played a vital role, with the theologically liberal Christians constituting an important element among those dissidents.

Since 1988, some evangelicals have come to recognize the socio-political responsibilities of Christianity and have attempted to put them into practice. In 1989 Kyung Suk Suh and his colleagues began to work for the realization of economic justice in Korean society. A group of young Christians under the leadership of Mahn Yol Yi and Jin Hong Kim began to publish *The Gospel and the Situation* from 1991, through which they have been trying to apply their faith to the political reality of their society. From 1990, Bong Ho Son and other evangelicals have been working for just elections.

Conclusion

Although there were a significant number of Christian politicians in the First Republic of Korea, they did not present a good witness. Including the President Syng Mahn Rhee, many Christian high officials in the government seemed to be more interested in maintaining their power and prestige than in applying their Christian faith and ethics to politics. As a result, the history of the First Republic of Korea, sometimes called a 'Christian Republic,' was stained by tyranny, corruption, and injustice.

Meanwhile, the Christian Church failed to play the prophetic role in relation to the state. It did not have a sense of responsibility as a watchman over the government. The Korean Church seemed to be satisfied with the fact that their President and many high government officials were professing Christians. Churches had a vague expectation that those Christian politicians would do much good for the Christian Church, and were grateful for the apparent measures that they accepted to be conducive to the "Christianization" of Korea. Therefore, they provided an uncritical support to Lee's government, even when it was committing serious injustices. Their thinking did not reach far enough to expect that Christian politicians should not only make religious gestures but also rule over the country according to biblical principles, viz., justice and righteousness.

Generally, the Church tended to show an opportunistic attitude toward the government. It seemed to flatter whoever grasped the power. The Church consistently praised Syng Mahn Rhee as a "great leader," a "patriotic hero," and even a Korean "Moses" so long as he was in power. After the April Revolution, the church newspapers began to criticize the already overthrown regime. They welcomed the military coup of Chung Hee Park enthusiastically and tended to justify the military coup as an 'inevitable' action for the country.

In the mid-sixties, for several years around the "normalization" controversy, conservative Korean Presbyterians did not show as much of a negative view toward Christian social responsibility. They were not dominated by the dualistic mentality that divided the "spiritual" from the "secular," nor did they teach that the Christian should obey the authorities unconditionally. On the contrary, they emphasized the Christian responsibility to be the "light" and "salt" in this world, as well as stressing the church's prophetic role in relation to the state.

From the late sixties onward, the conservative Presbyterian churches seemed to revoke all that they had said in the mid-sixties. They suddenly changed into passive supporters of the government. For such a change to have taken place, there must have been, at least to some extent, pressure and influence from the government in one way or other.

The first and the most serious mistake made by the conservative churches in the late sixties was their expressions of their support for Park's proposal for the amendment of the constitution in 1969. This mistake demonstrated the political naivete and the abject inability of the conservative church leaders to discern the hidden moral aspects at stake in the apparently political issues. This support also demonstrated the fact that 'spirituality' alone was not enough to equip a church leader for living in the world. Spiritual training, unaccompanied by training in the fields of the humanities and social sciences, was not enough to make a leader in the human community.

The point at which the conservative churches of Korea seemed to degenerate into spokesmen for the government was October 1972, when *The Christian Times* began to write articles in support of the Yushin constitution; the articles in *The Christian Times*, written to express the newspaper's political position during the Yushin period (1972 to 1979), will be recorded as the most shameful pages in the history of Korean Church.

During the seventies, the conservative churches totally failed to preach justice and to play the role of watchman over the state. Instead of standing with the weak, the poor and the oppressed of the society, they sided with the government, justifying the political leadership's attempt to prolong their reign by questionable means. Nevertheless, they called for the separation of church and state.

In summarizing the political witness of Korean conservative churches from 1945 to the late eighties, we can conclude that in general, they failed to perform their duty in relation to the state. To confess the failure of the conservative churches in exercising their socio-political responsibility should not be misunderstood, however, as an unquestioning praise of the liberal churches' line of political action. The liberal churches' pattern of political involvement was not ideal, although it is fair to say that they made a significant contribution to democratization and the development of justice in Korea.

But the theology of the liberal Christians departed from the traditional theology. At certain points it is questionable whether their religion contains the essential doctrines of Christianity or not. If not, their socio-political theories and actions fail to express genuine Christianity. Their political actions would be, at best, the work of a social movement, and their political theology a humanitarian system of social justice.

The liberal churches have been so preoccupied with politics that it is difficult to find in them the healthy balance between political witness and the other important duties of the Christian church. They seem to think that performing their political responsibility is all that is required of a church. Politics, however, should not be the only interest of the church.

One can also detect, from a Reformed perspective, a problem in rendering due obedience to the authorities on the part of the liberal churches. Granting that unconditional obedience to the authorities is not biblical, neither is it biblical for Christians to think lightly of them and too rashly reject the state's authority over them.

To ask the conservative Korean churches for a more faithful exercise of political discernment, then, is not to call for conformity to a more liberal pattern of political activism. It is to encourage those churches — and especially those of Reformed persuasion — to draw intentionally on the resources available in the study of past instances of Christian political faithfulness. We will now turn to the ways these resources can be utilized more effectively in a Reformed context.

1 *The Christian Times* began to be published in January of 1965. Before the Korean Presbyterian Church was divided into *Habdong* and *Tonghab* on the issue of World Council of Churches (hereafter, WCC), it had *The Christian News* as its denominational weekly newspaper. Therefore, until the division in 1959, the position of *The Christian New* can be said to stand for *Habdong* as well as for *Tonghab*. Since the division, however, *The Christian News* became *Tonghab*'s denominational paper. After the Division, *Habdong* did not have its own denominational paper until the publication of *The Christian Times* in 1965.

2 The political positions of other comparatively small Presbyterian denominations in Korea are almost the same as that of *Habdong,* since many of them were separated from it. Although the *Koshin* denomination has older history than the *Habdong*, its political position is also the same as that of the *Habdong*. In addition, as far as I researched, it was not possible to find any writing written by a *Koshin* scholar onthe issue of church and state or Christians and politics.

3 All translation from Korean to English here are my own.

4 Kyung Bae Min, *Church History of Korea* (Seoul: 1973), 372.

5 Young Jae Kim, "Political Actions and the Reformation Movement of the Korean Church After the Emancipation," *Shinhak Jinam*, 1985, No, 52-1, p. 94.

6 He was a Methodist and was later ordained as an elder. *The Christian News*, Jan. 15, 1956.

7 He received his B. A. at Harvard University and Ph.D. in political science at Princeton University.

8 Jong Goh Choi, *State and Religion* (Seoul: 1983), 193.

9 *The Christian Weekly*, June 9, 1948.

10 *Kidok Shinmoon*, Aug. 15, 1948.

11 Kyung Bae Min, 366.

12 *The Christian News*, August 4, 1952.

13 *Ibid.*

14 *Ibid.*

15 Jong Goh Choi, 196.

[16] Until his return to Korea in 1945, he spent several decades in America, so Lee had no support group in Korea, while his rivals were in a relatively favorable situation.

[17] Mahn Yol Yi, *Korean Christianity and the Historical Consciousness* (Seoul: 1981), 122.

[18] *The Christian News*, March 8, 1954.

[19] *Ibid*., May 28, 1956.

[20] *The Christian Times*, April 23, 1956.

[21] *Ibid.*

[22] *Ibid*., Dec. 24, 1956.

[23] Pyung Ik Kim, "Social Involvement of Korean Church," *Kidokgyo Sasang,* 69-6, p. 36.

[24] *The Christian News*, May 2, 1960.

[25] *The Christian News*, Aug. 22, 1960; April 24, 1961. *The Christian News* is a weekly newspaper published by *Tonghab* denomination, which is the largest Presbyterian Church in Korea advocating the ecumenism and supporting the WCC.

[26] Jong Ko Choi, 207.

[27] Mahn Yol Yi, 118-120.

[28] Hyon Sul Hong, "What has the Revolution brought to the Church?" *Kidokgyo Sasang,* 62-5.

[29] Bosun Yoon's father was an elder at Ahngookdong Church and his wife was an evangelist. *The Christian News,* Aug. 22, 1960.

[30] Ho Jin Kim, "Chung Hee Park's Leadership and the Strategy of Rule," *How to Understand the Modern Korean History* (Seoul; Dongah Ilbo Sa, 1990), 28.

[31] *Kidogkyo Sasang*, June 1961

[32] *The Christian News*, May 29, 1961.

[33] *The Christian News*, April 1, 1963.

[34] Yong Ho Kim, "the Republican Party and the Amendment of Constitution for the Third Presidential Term," *How to Understand the Modern Korean History* IV, 82.

[35] The decisive point was on the lawfulness of Japan's annexation of Korea. Concerning the date of the nullification of the treaties which led to the annexation of Korea into Japan, Koreans insisted that from the very outset of the Japanese invasion of Korea, the treaties were in-

valid, because they were made under the restraint and threat of force. Japan, however, maintained that those treaties were legally valid, and that therefore, they were nullified from August 15, 1945. Korean people were infuriated at the concession the Korean government made at this point. Because of this concession, the money Korea received from Japan became a grant-type aid instead of remuneration. Recently, it was reported that the treaties that led to the annexation of Korea did not meet the legal conditions and so, were invalid.

36 *The Christian Press,* July 9, 1965.

37 *The Christian Times,* July 12, 1965.

38 *Ibid*., July 19, 1965.

39 *Ibid*., June 21, 1965.

40 *Ibid*., April 19, 1969.

41 Yong Ho Kim, 102.

42 *Chosen Ilbo, Hangook Ilbo*, August 24, 1969.

43 KNCC; The Committee for Human Rights, *The Movement for the Democratization in 1970s, vol. 1* (Seoul: 1987), 81.

44 *Ibid*, 82.

45 Jong Go Choi, 224.

46 *The Movement for Democratization* vol. 1, 82.

47 *The Christian Times*, September 13, 1969.

48 *Dongah Ilbo*, April 26, 1971; *The Movement for the Democratization* vol. 1, 122.

49 Yong Ho Kim, 102.

50 On July 4, 1972, the South-North Joint Communique was announced by both governments of South and North Korea. According to which the secret messengers of both governments visited each other and began to talk about the reunification of Korea. The point of the communique was that both governments agreed to promote peace and endeavor to reunify Korea. This dialogue for reunification was stopped by both governments after each government amended the constitution to strengthen their reign. *The Movement for Democratization* vol. 1, 156-168.

51 *The Christian Times*, November 11, 1972.

52 *The Christian Times,* November 11, 1972.

53 *The Christian Times*, Nov. 18, 1972.

[54] *The Christian Times*, November 10, 17, 24, 1973.

[55] Chongshin Seminary is a conservative Presbyterian school that belongs to Habdong denomination which publishes *The Christian Times*.

[56] Ui Hwan Kim, "The Problem of Korean Church's Involvement in the Politics," *Shinhak Jinam* (March 1973): 25, 50.

[57] Ibid., 25, 28-30, 31-32. Kim does not mention, however, the statement, "Our Position on the Amendment of the Constitution," which was issued in Sep. 1969 by the conservative denominations to support Chung Hee Park's desire to extend his term. Nor does he blame the extremely political serial "The Necessity of the 'Yushin' Constitution" published in his denominational newspaper in previous month.

[58] *Ibid.*, 28.

[59] Ibid., 50, 25, 27.

[60] Bong Ho Son, "The Problem of Christian Social Ethics,"*Shinhak Jinam* 1974, No. 41-3, p. 85.

[61] *Ibid.*, 87.

[62] *Ibid.*, 104.

[63] Bong Ho Son, "Mission and the Social Justice," *Shinhak Jinam* 74, No. 41-4, pp. 70-71.

[64] *Ibid.*, 67-68.

[65] *Ibid.*, 69-70.

[66] *Ibid.*, 71.

[67] *The Christian Times*, November 16, 1974.

[68] *The Movement for Democratization* vol. 1, 506-8.

[69] *The Christian Times*, "A Proclamation on the Present Situation by Anti-communist Christians," December 7, 1974.

[70] *Ibid.*, November 30, 1974.

[71] *Ibid.*, November 30, 1974.

[72] *Ibid.*, December 7, 1974.

[73] *The Movement for the Democratization* vol. 1, 581.

[74] *The Christian Times*, February 1, 1975.

[75] *Ibid.*, February 15, 1975.

[76] *Ibid.*, April 26, 1975.

CHAPTER VI

THE PROPHETIC RESPONSIBILITY OF THE KOREAN CHURCH

The previous chapters have clearly revealed that there is a serious gap between the political ideas and practices in the Reformed tradition and those of the Korean Presbyterian Church. This has been especially true of the Korean attitude toward politics, Christian political responsibility and unjust political authorities. What caused Korean Presbyterians to estrange themselves from the Reformed tradition concerning those issues? The misunderstanding seems to relate to the following themes: the concept of separation of church and state, the intent of Romans 13:1-7, the right and duty of resistance to unjust civil authorities, and finally, the relationship between politics and the Christian religion. This chapter aims at explaining each of these aspects and making some corrective suggestions.

Separation of Church and State

Korean Presbyterians often treat it as a biblical truth that church and state should be separated. By the term "the separation of church and state," they mean not only that the state should not interfere with the religious affairs of the church, but also that the church should never speak to the government and never express its opinion concerning socio-political issues. In a word, they believe that the church should never pronounce its position on any issues other than "purely" spiritual matters. They believe that political matters and religious matters are always clear-cut.

This is to take the term "separation of church and state" too literally. It is to ignore where that term came from or in what historical background that term was formulated. Since this issue has received much attention in the North American setting, it will be useful to explore the lessons to be learned from that discussion.

The constitution of the United States, as enacted in 1789, had no specific provision for the separation of Church and State. It was at first thought that no further limitation on the powers of the new central body, the U.S. Congress, should be added, since it was held that the Congress could have only such powers as had been conferred upon it, either by the people as individuals, or by the sovereign States. Nonetheless, many people feared leaving the question of religious liberty to mere implication, and so a series of ten Amendments, termed the Bill of Rights, were added to the U.S. Constitution in 1791.[1] What is called the "separation of Church and State" originated from the First Amendment: "Congress shall make no law respecting an establishment of religion, or prohibiting the free exercise thereof."

There has been a heated debate among scholars as to exactly what was intended by the Establishment Clause. What did the framers of this clause mean by it? What was their original intent in inserting it? There are two answers to this question: one provides a broader interpretation of the clause, whereas the other, a narrower interpretation. The broader interpretation is most authoritatively represented by the statement of the United States Supreme Court in *Everson v. Board of Education* in 1947. Justice Hugo Black, speaking for the majority, declared:

> The "establishment of religion" clause of the First Amendment means at least this: Neither a state nor the Federal Government can set up a church. Neither can pass laws which aid one religion, aid all religions, or prefer one religion over another. Neither can force nor influence a person to go to or to remain away from church against his will or force him to profess a belief or disbelief in any religion....No tax in any amount, large or small, can be levied to support any religious activities or institutions....Neither a state nor the Federal Government, can, openly or secretly, participate in the affairs of any religious organizations or groups and vice versa.

As is clearly seen above, even those who interpret the First Amendment most broadly understand it to refer to the ban of government aid of religion, including establishing a church.[2] In other words, by this amendment, the religious liberty of every individual was secured. From that time on, religion was supposed to be a matter of purely private decision. The state did not have the right to interfere with the realm of religion and the conscience of an individual citizen. The First Amendment no longer allowed the government to decide for the citizens which religion was the best for them.

The second or narrower interpretation of the Establishment Clause holds that the clause had the sole purpose of preventing government from allowing a single state church to have preference over other churches. According to this interpretation, the members of the First Congress understood "establishment of religion" as "a formal, legal union of a single church or religion with government giving the one church or religion an exclusive position of power and favor over all other churches or denominations."[3] Advocates of this view reject the contention that every form of public aid or support for religion is prohibited. They argue that under certain circumstances the government can provide support to religions on a nondiscriminatory basis.

No matter which interpretation is correct, one thing is clear: the phrase "separation of church and state" in its historical context has nothing to do with a ban on the church to express its ethical concern on socio-political issues, particularly when those issues significantly affect the course of the nation and have moral implications.

To better understand the historical context of the Establishment Clause, we need to further examine the American experience with the establishment of religion in its colonial period.[4] The early settlers in New England held to the belief, common in their day, that the establishment of religion was both right and necessary. The idea of a national church was firmly fixed in their minds, and the concept of tolerating all sects did not yet exist. As Puritans who were decisively influenced by Calvin's theology, they accepted Calvin's principle on the relation of church and state. In the last chapter of his *Institutes* which discusses civil government, Calvin averred that it had "as its appointed end...to cherish and protect the outward worship of God, to defend sound doctrine of piety and the position of the Church." In other words, he insisted that the civil government had "the duty of rightly establishing religion." His claim that the government was "far more excellent" than bread, water, sun, and air was based on its protection of "the true religion" from idolatry, sacrilege, blasphemies and other public offenses.[5] The New England Puritans were people who left England with a dream to establish such a Calvinistic relationship between church and state.

Calvin, however, was not the inventor of the concept of the national church. After the Roman Emperor Theodosius's Edict, for more than one thousand years, the concept of religious pluralism did not exist. There could be only one "true" religion. If not, the medieval people feared that there would be chaos. The truth was only one, and therefore, the true church also was only one. The Reformation made no immediate change in the theory that all the citizens of a nation should be of the same religion. This was accepted by the Reformers as strongly as by their opponents.

One state, one religion, was the principle almost universally accepted. In central Europe the religion of the prince was supposed to be the religion of the people, and dissent from the religion he professed would be no more tolerated by him than would rebellion against his laws.[6] The experience of the English Puritans before immigrating to New England was no exception. They knew no other than the establishment in England, and accordingly, they established Congregationalism in New England.

The Cambridge Platform, a document adopted in 1648 by a synod of the Massachusetts churches, shows what the nature of the establishment was in New England. According to the Platform, the civil authorities were supposed to protect the "true church" by maintaining both tablets of the Decalogue. They had the right to punish religious violations such as "Idolatry, Blasphemy, Heresy, venting corrupt and pernicious opinions, that destroy the Foundation, open contempt of the Word preached, profanation of the Lord's Day, disturbing the peaceable administration and exercise of the worship and holy things of God, and the like...." For the New England Puritans "atheism was considered as heinous as murdering; idolatry, as bad as adultery; profanity, as grave an offense as theft; and Sabbath-breaking was as far beyond the pale as was perjury."[7]

Thus the establishment of religion in America until the time of the framing of the Bill of Rights had meant government aid and sponsorship of some churches. Financial support of the churches came principally from taxes levied on all taxpayers. This kind of establishment lasted until 1833 in Massachussets, and until 1818 in Connecticut.[8]

According to Kik, four main factors had worked to effect a drastic change in the relation of church and state in America. The first is the English Act of Toleration which was enacted in 1689. Through this act, for the first time in the history of England, the worship of God was legally permitted outside of the established church. Although it did not bring the Nonconformists complete freedom of religion, after that those who did not attend the state-supported church were exempt from civil penalties. This Act exercised a great influence on the measure of toleration in colonial America.

The second and more important factor involved the influx of immigrants from Europe. With each group having their own religion, which led to the creation of such a wide variety of denominations, it became practically impossible to maintain ecclesiastical conformity. In the colonies where there was an established church, the dissenters pressed hard for religious freedom, and they redoubled their efforts when there was some attempt to establish an Anglican episcopate.

The third factor was the struggle of the non-Anglican Protestants for toleration in Virginia. There the Church of England was strongly entrenched as the established church. In this colony, discrimination against other denominations was a matter of common policy. Congregational ministers who came to the Virginia colony in 1642 were ordered to leave. Baptists were fined or imprisoned for holding unauthorized meetings. Presbyterians, along with other dissenters, were taxed for the support of the state church. In 1760, Baptists submitted the first petition for religious freedom to the Virginia House of Burgesses. The time was not yet ripe, however, for the reception and passing of this petition.

Lastly, the American Revolution had the effect of raising not only the question of political liberty but that of religious liberty as well. The presbytery of Hanover petitioned the Virginia House of Burgessess to dissolve the alliance of church and state and to allow the free exercise of religion according to the dictates of one's conscience. The presbytery argued that the Gospel asked for the support of only its own adherents; therefore, it did not need state aid. This petition was supported by Thomas Jefferson and James Madison. Madison drafted the Bill for Establishing Religious Freedom, which he ranked next to the Declaration of Independence. This bill was enacted into law in 1785 under the leadership of Madison.

When we place the First Amendment in this larger picture of history, the original intent of the concept of "separation of Church and State" becomes much more clearly understandable. It intended the abolishment of the state's support of particular churches or church. That is to say, the American pattern of separation of church and state has never meant that churches should not express ethical concern about society. It does not mean that church and state may not cooperate with one another, nor that the state is exempt from the moral law wherewith God sets the bounds of justice for nations as well as individuals, nor does it require the separation of civic duty and religious faith. It has meant, instead, that church and state are mutually free, and that neither may rightfully control the other.

Besides the tradition of establishment, there might have been one more factor that led to the constitutional guarantee of the "separation of church and state." To secure the church's independence in purely ecclesiastical matters also seems to have served as a motive for the formation of the

First Amendment. Calvin, who is alleged to have instituted a theocracy in Geneva, insisted on the separation of church and state in some respects. With all his advocacy of the government support for the "true church," he did not allow the government "to make laws according to its own decision concerning religion and the worship of God."[9] His intention was to protect the Church from the control of the political order since caesaropapism or erastianism was a common phenomenon in the European countries during the sixteenth-century.

At that time the state often intruded into the realms of the church. For example, in sixteenth-century England, which was the immediate background of the American Puritans, the Crown gained a great deal of control over the English Church. The monarchs claimed that "procedures concerning taxation, appointment, appeals, and punishment of the clergy fell under their hegemony." Claiming to be the 'Supreme Head of the Church,' they possessed a superior sacerdotal power in selecting the bishops and demanded from all bishops homage and fealty as "important civil servants of the Crown."[10] As a result, nominees of the king usually filled the bishoprics as well as many minor benefices. Very few appeals could go from English courts to the papal curia without the king's permission. Moreover, the kings prosecuted the heretics in the civil courts. As a result of this regal control over the ecclesiastical affairs, both the independence of the church and the religious liberty of the individuals were seriously threatened. This historical experience of the Puritan ancestors might well have influenced the Founding Fathers when they were framing the First Amendment.

By any analysis, the emphasis was not laid upon preventing the church from expressing its ethical concern about public affairs. For it appealed to the consciences of the rulers and the people without having any legally-binding power. Thomas G. Sanders notes that the Massachussets Puritans already insisted on "a separation of political and religious offices" in the sense that "the same person could not hold an important office in both church and state."[11] Nevertheless, a nineteenth-century scholar on Puritan society could write: "...to this day [1844] in no other country is the legitimate influence of the clergy in public affairs —an influence derived from their intelligence, united with religion, virtue, and public spirit—more manifest, or salutary, than in New England."[12]

In 1952, the U. S. Supreme Court stated, in a decision which upheld the New York State system of released-time religious education (Zorach case): "The First Amendment, however, does not say that in every and all respect there shall be separation of Church and State." In fact, churches of most traditions in America have made a regular practice of speaking on public issues. Particularly, U. S. Presbyterians "have been deeply involved in political action throughout the history of the nation....they have sought to change its direction through the use of petitions, boycotts, public demonstrations, lobbying for specific bills, and backing particular political candidates."[13] In view of this reality, we can safely infer that the First Amendment to the United States Constitution intended a legal and institutional separation between church and state. It never meant a moral or a spiritual separation. The conviction of the American Calvinists has always been that since religion and public life were inextricably interwined, the church has the right and responsibility to express its ethical concerns in the political orders.[14]

The Problem of Romans 13:1-7

Many Korean Presbyterians refer to Romans 13:1-7 as the basis of their political quietism. If the Scripture tells them to obey the rulers, even Roman emperors such as Nero, who tyrannically persecuted the Christians, then it is not lawful for Christians to disobey or resist the government, even an unjust one. Moreover, they assert that the church should avoid expressing any criticism of the government. In their view, Romans 13:1-7 is a divine call for an unconditional and unquestioning obedience to whatever government that might be in power.

Does Romans 13:1-7 really teach that? Have Calvinists of the past and the present interpreted that passage in that way? The answer is that they have not treated the Romans passage as a mandate to political passivity. We will outline here some Calvinist observations on this passage.

First, verse one of chapter 13, shows that the origin of political authority teaches that the authority of the human government is not absolute: "There is no authority except from God." God is the source of civil authority. He ordained the political institutions: "Thrones or dominions or principalities or authorities—all things were created through him and for him" (Colossians 1:16-17). As Francis A. Schaeffer puts it, the authority of the state is "a delegated" one; it is not "autonomous." Therefore, Schaeffer goes on: "The civil government, as all of life, stands under the Law of God."[15] It was remarkable that in a time when the Roman Emperors were claiming to be the ultimate authority, Paul could "relativize" the Roman imperial order. When the emperors were setting themselves up as deities, Paul responded to them, "No, the empire is not sovereign," only God is sovereign.[16]

Secondly, this passage teaches that the civil authorities are God's "servants." They have a specific duty, the promotion of justice and the welfare of society: "...rulers are not a terror to good conduct, but to bad," (v. 3) and "...are God's servants for the good of the people"(v. 4). That is to say that there is an "inherent limitation" in the power of the rulers.[17] The powers are not given for the authorities to wield arbitrarily and misuse it for their own self-gratification. In ordaining the authorities, God had a specific purpose: the implementation of justice by executing "God's wrath on the wrong doers" (v. 4).

It can be affirmed, therefore, that by introducing the *raison d'etre* of the governing authorities, this passage connotes the basis of legitimacy of the political authorities. The authority which performs its duty faithfully is legitimate. On the contrary, when it fails to do its duty, it is no longer regarded as a legitimate authority; it degenerates into an illegitimate one. In Schaeffer's formulation:

> Since God ordained the state to be an agent of justice, to restrain evil and to protect the good in society, when it does the reverse, it has no proper authority. It is then a usurped authority and as such it becomes lawless and is tyranny. [18]

Hence the "Calvinist consensus" that this passage is never to be abused by sanctioning tyranny by absolute rulers.[19] It is never a *carte blanche* given to tyrants. James Dunn, a respected New Testament scholar asserts:

> where a government was not serving God for the good of its citizens, any appeal to this passage as a way of maintaining their subservience would be a complete distortion and an abuse both of Paul's purpose and of its continuing Scriptural significance.[20]

Thirdly, verse 5 implies the possibility of Christian disobedience to the government, for it states that Christians should obey the authorities "for the sake of conscience." As Stephen Mott rightly indicates: "From the fact that conscience is to be a motivating force in obeying government, a basis may be inferred for disobeying government when its actions are not in conformity with the voice of informed conscience."[21] The English Puritans believed that the authorities who betrayed their duty ceased to be a legitimate authority and in that case the people were no longer under obligation to obey them. Typical of the Puritan divines is the comment on Romans 13 made by William Bridge who frequently preached before the Long Parliament and was in the assembly of divines at Westminster:

> Because the power that every soul is here commanded to be subject to, and not to resist, is that power which is not a terror to good works but to evil....and therefore the subjection commanded, and resistance forbidden, is not in things that are unlawful, and contrary to the law of God....and the minister thereof is the ordinance of God to us for good...but when he commands a things unlawful, and contrary to the law of God, he is not the minister of God to us for good,therefore in this scripture there is no such thing commanded us to be subject to, and not to resist the ungodly command of princes.[22]

Calvinists have never been easy "subjects" for the tyrants to handle. They have always judged the governing of civil authorities in the light of the Word of God. In fact, the history of the church, particularly that of the Calvinist church, has been "invariably one of questioning, challenging and redefining the political order....the mere existence of the church...kept alive the idea of limits on state power and provided the base for the growth of modern constitutional government."[23] As Francis Schaeffer pointed out: "In almost every place where the Reformed had success there was some form of civil disobedience or armed rebellion." Examples are Netherlands, Denmark, Germany, Switzerland, Geneva, Scotland, Hungary, France, and Spain.[24]

A Bottom Line

For Schaeffer there was a "bottom line." "At a certain point," he argued, "there is not only the right, but the duty, to disobey the state."[25] For this conclusion, he draws on Samuel Rutherford's *Lex Rex: or The Law and the Prince*. Rutherford (1600-1661) was a Scottish Presbyterian minister who later became Rector at St. Andrews University in Scotland. He was one of the most influential Scottish commissioners at the Westminster Assembly of Divines (1643-7). In *Lex Rex*, published in 1644, Rutherford discussed what the proper Christian response should be to nonbiblical acts by the state. Since he attacked the undergirding foundation of the seventeenth century political government in Europe—"the divine right of kings"—his treatise was outlawed in both England and Scotland. The parliament of Scotland met in order to condemn Rutherford to death for his views. The only reason he was not executed as a civil rebel was because he died first. The points of *Lex Rex* observed by Francis Schaeffer can be summarized as follows.[26]

The doctrine of "the divine right of kings" held that the king or state ruled as God's appointed regent. This being so, the king's word was law. In Rutherford's view, however, the basic premise of civil government, that is, law, must be based on God's law as given in the Bible: the state had to be administered according to the principles of God's Law. If the law was based on God's law, all humans, even the king, were under the law and not above it. The law was king, and if the king and the government disobeyed the law, they were to be disobeyed. Acts of the state which contradicted God's Law were illegitimate and acts of tyranny.

According to Rutherford, tyranny was defined as ruling without the sanction of God. A power to oppress was not from God, and was not a power, but a licentious deviation of a power from sinful nature and "the old serpent." Since tyranny was Satanic, not to resist it was to resist God. Conversely, to resist tyranny was to honor God. Furthermore, since the ruler was granted power conditionally, the people had the power to withdraw their sanction if the proper conditions were not fulfilled.

A ruler, however, was not to be deposed merely because he committed a single breach of the compact he had with the people. Only when the magistrate was attacking the fundamental structure of society was he to be relieved of his power and authority. In other words, if the state was deliberately committed to destroying its ethical commitment to God, then resistance to it was appropriate.

For the private person, there were three levels of resistance: first, he/she must defend himself by protest; second, he/she must flee if at all possible; third, he/she may use force, if necessary, to defend himself/herself. When the state committed illegitimate acts against a corporate body—such as duly constituted a state or local body, or even a church, there were two levels of resistance; remonstration (or protest) and then, if necessary, force employed in self-defence. Resistance to the state had to be under the protection of the duly constituted authorities, that is, the lesser magistrates (local officials).

In *A Christian Manifesto*, which Schaeffer professes to have written under the decisive influence of *Lex Rex,* he asserts that Christians need not reject the use of force indiscriminately. "If there is a legitimate reason for the use of force," he declares, "and if there is a vigilant precaution against its overaction in practice, then at a certain point a use of force is justifiable." For Schaeffer, the proper use of force was not exclusively the province of the state. Such an assumption, born of "naivete," left us "without remedy when and if the state takes on totalitarian dimensions."[27] Therefore, a "bottom line" was needed: "If there is no final place for civil disobedience, then the government has been made autonomous, and as such, it has been put in the place of the living God."[28]

Puritans and Revolution

Schaeffer also argues that the American Declaration of Independence in 1776 contains many elements of the Reformation thinking of John Knox and Rutherford. Therefore, it should be carefully considered in the discussion of resistance. It spoke directly to the responsibility of citizens concerning oppressive civil government. After recognizing the human being's God-given rights, the Declaration went on to declare that whenever civil government became destructive of these rights, "it is the right of the people to alter and abolish it, and institute new government, laying its foundation on such principles, and organizing its powers in such form, as to them shall seem most likely to effect their safety and happiness."[29] The Founding Fathers cautioned in the Declaration that the established government should not be altered or abolished for "light and transient causes." But when there is a "long train of abuses and usurpations" designed to produce an oppressive, authoritarian state, "it is their right, it is their duty, to throw off such government." The United States could not have been established, contends Schaeffer, if the Founding Fathers had not realized that there is a "bottom line."[30]

Besides Schaeffer, numerous historians have noted the strong religious influence on the American Revolution. In his book *Christians in American Revolution*, Mark Noll affirmed that "...vast numbers of

American Christians offered wholehearted support to the movement leading to separation from Great Britain." In particular,

> the direct descendants of Anglo-American Puritanism, Congregationalists and Presbyterians, distinguished themselves in defense of colonial prerogatives. To some observers, in fact, colonial patriots took on the appearance of religious crusaders.[31]

Even their opponents recognized that the Presbyterians were the leading group of the American Revolution: a Hessian captain wrote of his experiences in Pennsylvania, "call this war...by whatever name you may, only call it not an American Rebellion, it is nothing more or less than an Irish-Scotch Presbyterian Rebellion."[32] Particularly, American clergy were a "primary factor" in the American Revolution and their support led to their being called the "black regiment" of the revolution.[33]

Not only in the American Revolution but in the English Revolution of the 1640s, the Puritan clergy played a significant role from the start. As is affirmed by Christopher Hill, a social and economic historian on this period, Puritanism was "perhaps the most important complex of ideas that prepared the people's mind for revolution."[34] Puritanism first began as a clerical movement and later it became a full-blown revolutionary army of gentry and yeomen, parliamentarians and people, who brought down the Stuart monarchy and began the commonwealth era.[35] The passion of the Puritan clergy "to remake society" was manifested in a sermon of a Puritan minister preached before the House of Commons in 1641:

> Reformation must be universal...Reform all places, all persons and callings; Reform the benches of judgements, the inferior magistrates...that judgement may run down like a stream, and justice like many waters. Reform the church, go into the temple (the Lord is gone before you) and as he hath done, so do you, overthrow the tables of these money changers, whip out them that buy and sell, that buy living and sell souls....[36]

Before the Christian who was swallowed up by the zeal for God, nothing could be exempt from reformation. Everything had to be restored to the original form as was intended by God and his Word. "Reform the universities...." Thomas Case went on,

> Reform the cities, reform the countries, reform inferior schools of learning, reform the Sabbath, reform the ordinances, the worship of God...you have

> more work to do than I can speak...Every plant which my heavenly father hath not planted shall be rooted up.[37]

Thus, the Puritans became the first group in history to understand that one could intentionally and organizationally make changes in one's community. They combined the passion for the sovereignty of God over all of life with the conviction that the fruits of conversion were relevant to the reconstruction of the social order.[38] As Noll describes it:

> The Puritan perspective, first of all, saw life as a whole. Puritanism did not separate social, ecclesiastical, and theological concerns. Its comprehensive point of view saw religious significance in public acts and public significance in religious acts....Since the battle between good and evil, between God and Satan, was carried into every aspect of life, decisions in the communal life of the wider society had a moral significance equal to those enacted within the narrow confines of the church.[39]

One of the Puritan political ideas that made a decisive contribution to the theory of popular resistance to tyrants was that God delegated the political power to the rulers through the people. In other words, Puritans believed that people were the first seat and receptacle of civil power. In his "Tenure of Kings and Magistrates," Milton wrote:

> ...The power of kings and magistrates is nothing else but what is only derivative, transferred and committed to them in trust from the people, to the common good of them all, in whom the power yet remains fundamentally, and cannot be taken from them, without a violation of their natural birthright.[40]

For Milton, it was not only that the authority was derived from the people, but also it was "both originally and naturally for their good in the first place" and not for the good of the king or magistrate. Therefore, "as oft as they shall judge it for the best," the people had the right "either [to] choose him or reject him, retain him or depose him...."[41]:

Already a century earlier, some Puritan ministers were already making exactly the same point. For example, Christopher Goodman, a Marian exile and friend of John Knox, wrote in his radical treatise, *How Superior Powers Ought to Be Obeyed:*

> When kings or rulers become blasphemous of God, oppressor and murderers of their subjects, they ought no more to be accounted kings or lawful magistrates, but as private men to be examined, accused, condemned and

> punished by the law of God to which thy are and ought to be subject, and being convicted and punished by that law, it is not man's but God's doing....[42]

In these Puritan political ideas, we find the embryos of some fundamental principles of modern democracy: popular sovereignty, the concept of social contract, and the right of the impeachment of the civil authorities.

Historically, most Calvinists in every country thought that forceful resistance to the tyrannical government was not absolutely unbiblical. Rather, as we have seen in chapters 1 and 2, much of the resistance theory was developed and applied by direct followers of John Calvin. To name just some, John Ponet, Christopher Goodman, John Knox, Theodore Beza, Samuel Rutherford, and Mornay were all major figures who made a significant contribution to the development of resistance theory.

Modern Reformed theologians also tend to recognize that revolution is legitimate under certain circumstances. They usually suggest six conditions for the revolution to be legitimate: 1) The cause must be just, 2) It should be the last resort, 3) It should be led by a lawful authority, 4) There should be a reasonable hope of victory, 5) A due proportion should exist between the good that may probably be accomplished and the probable evil effect, 6) It should be rightly conducted through the use of right means.[43]

The Prophetic Duty of the Church

Is it desirable and biblical that the official church make statements on socio-political issues? Some Christians are strongly opposed to it on the ground that such an action of the church is "interfering with politics." They resent Christian assemblies, or the clergy, and especially the representatives of a denomination expressing in public any views on political, social, or economic problems. They believe that it is not proper for citizens of the Heavenly city to be involved in the controversies of earthly affairs. So they say, "Let the Church care for the souls of men and the State, for their bodies," or "Let the Church mind the things of God, and the politicians the things of Caesar."

Some Christians fear that the authority of the church might be undermined by the church's expression of their views on public matters. Since the church lacks a professional understanding of sociology, political science and economics, they argue, its statements can be found to be wrong, premature or too late, misinformed, or naive. Consequently, people may lose confidence in the church's ability to lead them in the spiritual realm. In other words, because of the church's involvement in the social affairs, its witness is damaged in the area of life which ultimately counts.

Some evangelicals complain that when the church takes a stand, it breaks the unity of the church. Since there will certainly be people in the church who do not agree with the thrust of the pronouncement of the church, they fear, it splits the church into opposing groups.

Reformed Christians, however, believe that Christianity is the religion of the incarnation and is, therefore, concerned with the whole of human nature. "A platonic concept of spirituality which does not include all of life is not true biblical spirituality. True spirituality touches all of life, including things of government and law, and not just 'religious things.'"[44] If there is a church which is indifferent to the cry of undernourished children, the unhappiness and discomfort of the multitudes who do not have decent homes, the stunted lives of those who are below the poverty line, and the sense of frustration which comes from prolonged unemployment, and which still thinks of itself as "spiritual," one may well wonder what kind of "spirituality" this is.

Reformed Christians argue that to speak of any social issues, the church need not be the best authority in that field. As an institution entrusted with the goals and values which should guide the destiny of humankind, it has the ethical standard and principles it learned from the Bible. It is concerning those aspects of morality underlying the apparently secular affairs that the church wants to speak.

Of course there are dangers. Sometimes the church's statement could prove mistaken, if it is issued without completely knowing the inside story. That is inevitable to some extent. But it will serve as a means of witness to let people know that the church does care.[45] Reformed Christians believe that if the church fails to throw the weight of the corporate church against modern-day social evils, the witness of the church is seriously harmed.[46]

Reformed Christians believe that the church's expression of its social concern prompts the laity to become interested in social affairs. In effect, the church's declarations are meant to stimulate, instruct and direct individual Christians on controversial social issues.[47]

Reformed thinkers believe that the existence of a variety of opinions on one issue does not threaten the unity of the church. For them, "unity does not mean uniformity." Davies puts it nicely:

> If the church, following in the steps of its master it must expect conflict. To avoid this on the grounds of preserving some supposed unity is to pretend that there can be a unity which accepts injustice, and that this is a harmony, while it is no more than a not entirely overt combat between exploiter and exploited—it is to say peace, peace, when there is no peace (Jer. 6:14).

The official church has a prophetic duty. The prophets in the Old Testament proclaimed that the righteous God demanded justice and mercy from his people. They condemned social injustice, the intrigues of the statesmen, the greed of the powerful in accumulating wealth, the callousness of the rich who ground the faces of the poor, the covetousness of the landlord who added field to field, and the luxury of the upper-class in over-indulging in drink and food at their banquets.

Also it is of value to the state that over against it there should be a church which has the right both to exhort and warn it to follow in the ways of righteousness, truth and mercy. When the state neglects the mandate of justice, it is the church's duty to call the state back to its proper role. Therefore, the state must stand back so as to give the church freedom to criticize and exhort.

When a denomination, or an ecumenical organization, comes to a consensus on a public matter, their representatives may bring that consensus to the attention of the agencies of government. This may involve testimony before legislative committees, communications to the President, or meetings with representatives of executive departments.

It would be wrong, however, for the church to issue pronouncements rashly and irresponsibly without taking the time to become informed as much as possible about the issue in question. Once it chooses to be involved, it must play the role well. The statements of the church should prove to be right at least most of the time when they take stand. "If silence due to apathy is one form of sin, overzealous pronouncements are the other side of the same coin."[48]

In other words, it is better for the churches to be silent than to make casual and uninformed statements on complicated subjects. The effectiveness of the churches' statement depends on economy in their use — if the church acts and speaks too often there will be diminishing returns. The church should be very cautious about committing itself as a church to any position that is controversial.

Nevertheless, if, as is the case with Korean conservative Presbyterian churches during the last several decades, the churches never act or speak on matters of public morality which seriously affect the life of the people, this would be a sign not of restraint, but of indifference or an escape from assuming responsibility for the fate of the nation.

While the official Church should both proclaim the principles of Christian morality and show their application to society, it should not attempt to work out detailed programs of political and social reform. If the Church is to concern itself with political issues, it must do so mainly in the interests of morals and righteousness. Churches as organizations and Christian leaders whose chief area of competence is theology or Christian ethics should show self-restraint in suggesting detailed answers to the socio-political problems and not lay down the law on issues which are largely technical or which involve strategic judgements for which there is no Christian wisdom.

It is important that we draw a distinction between the political actions of the church in its official and corporate capacity, and those of groups and individuals belonging to it. While political action on the part of the official church should be strictly limited, individual members of, or specific groups within, the church may rightly advocate some specific program or policy. Within the church there should be men and women who have studied carefully the urgent problems of the day, and are able to speak with authority on them. Groups of clergy and laity should specialize in international or social questions so as to give informed guidance to their church and the nation. When making public the conviction they have reached and when pressing them upon the electorate, they are not committing the whole Church, but they are educating it as well as helping to awaken the conscience of the whole community. The statements that are made by various commissions officially created by the churches and empowered to speak for themselves do not have the authority of the churches behind them. Members of the churches who disagree are not committed to them. They have only the weight that is given to them by the authority of the persons involved and by the intrinsic merit of the statements. This is a well-tested scheme and the least vulnerable to criticism.

Is a Christian Party Necessary?

Advocating the formation of Christian political groups does not necessarily mean advocating a Christian political party. Many scholars who have examined the options of Christian political involvement are skeptical about the necessity of a Christian party. The chief reason for their suspicion toward such a suggestion is that if there should develop "Christian politics" of a partisan sort, the church would be identified with a Christian party. In that case, the influence of the church would be limited to one party. Moreover, the church's fate will be significantly dependent on the fortunes of any political movement. Though the church benefits by the success of a Christian party, it will suffer with it by its defeat. Besides, the more vigorous its political advocacy is, the more enemies the church will create. The enemy will consider the church as a political enemy to be weakened and injured.

From the history of the medieval church which claimed temporal power, we can assume that the church would lose spiritual influence if it either commits itself to one of the existing parties or forms a party of its own. In winning political victories, it may lose its spiritual authority. "At the height of its political power, it may be at the lowest ebb in spiritual influence. Political work is very engrossing, and calls for time and care if it is to be effective. The time spent on perfecting the political machine may be secured at the cost of other and far more important duties."[49]

Paul Marshall does not think there is any "in principle" reason for Christians not to form their own party.[50] "It is certainly not forbidden by the gospel and it could become necessary." The reasons for his lack of enthusiasm about the idea of a Christian party are practical ones. "With present realities," he declares, a Christian party would be "quixotic or ideological." To be worthwhile, it would require an "alienation from present parties and a widespread Christian political consciousness." These conditions do not exist now, however. Hence it is doubtful that such a party would be useful in realizing any authentic Christian goals in the near future.

The Problem of Negative Attitude toward Politics

It seems urgent for the conservative Korean Christians to reflect on whether their attitude toward politics is really as "Reformed" or

"Calvinistic" as they claim it to be. The truth seems the opposite. Many of their leaders, including those who agree on the necessity of social reform, have a sixteenth-century Anabaptist understanding of politics which Calvin severely reproached.

Bong Ho Son, one of the representative Christian thinkers in the conservative Presbyterian Church of Korea, shows a very negative and resigned attitude toward politics and the state. Perhaps too much disillusioned by Korean politics, he came to think that politics and political order themselves are inherently evil. Politics are "morally ambiguous," and "unholy," and they cannot be "harmonized with the holiness which the Church is in pursuit of."

For Bong Ho Son, the state also is far from being a divine institution with a sacred mission. Rather, it is a "fundamentally immoral" institution that expresses the "collective economic selfishness of the people." Therefore, he argues, when Christians participate in it, their "hands are defiled": they might have to "compromise with the evil."[51] Christians had better not "expect anything desirable from politics or politicians."[52]

In spite of this negative understanding of politics and the state, Son insists that the Church and the clergy should not be indifferent to the political order. As citizens of the state, he asserts, Christians, including the clergy, should assume responsibility for all of the state. The Church has a duty to make the state moral.[53] It must do its prophetic duty by warning the state of its immorality and exhorting the powerful to use their power "in a righteous way." In addition, Son contends that the individual Christians, not the Church, have the duty of practicing politics "in a Christian way."[54]

Here lies the puzzle regarding Son's viewpoint. If, as he maintains, politics are inherently evil, and the state is immoral by nature, how can one be involved in politics and remain just and clean? Is it not, as Monsma shrewdly pointed out, like asking a girl to be engaged in prostitution and nevertheless to perform her job in a clean or just way?[55]

As was discussed in chapters 1 and 2, the view of Calvin and his followers on politics and the state was never negative. For them, the government was a divinely ordained institution for the implementation of justice and the "good" of the citizens. The magistracy, for Calvin, was the most sacred and the most honorable calling of all. Calvin relentlessly reproved the Anabaptists as "fanatics" because they condemned politics and the political order. In fact, Calvinism always has been characterized by its positive view of politics and the political order. In view of this, the conservative Korean Presbyterian Churches can be said to have been estranged from one of the most important Reformed traditions: the concern for politics and society.

In the modern world the power of the state has been vastly expanded. In the past, the functions of the state were limited to the negative sides: suppressing disorders, violence, injustice and crime. Today, the emphasis is also laid upon its positive duties. In addition to the protection of the weak, it is also to provide for the well-being of all of its citizens. The state is supposed to secure their food, houses, education, recreation and work under favorable conditions, etc. It should care for them "from the cradle to the grave." In order for the state to do all the duties imposed upon it, it is inevitable that it should have at its disposal unprecedented power.

On the other hand, the state has a tremendous potential for evil. The political decisions made by the government can be fatal for millions of people. Through compulsory education, a controlled press, cinema, a network of police and spies, it can mold the minds and control the actions of its citizens. Government itself can be an evil structure beholden to the already privileged in society. As Revelation 13 suggests, the state can be a terrible instrument of Satan.

Under these conditions, if Christians take no part in politics, they are handing the state over to the secularists and atheists. When the state notices that the church has no interest in political issues which imply the dimension of justice, it will feel free to rule arbitrarily and oppressively, confident that it will meet no opposition. Thus, it is essential that Christians do all they can to maintain government as an agency of justice and to prevent it from degenerating into a tyrannical power. The church should be the last bastion of justice and conscience in society. If even the church betrays this responsibility, no hope will be left in that society.

Love and Political Action

The Greatest Commandment of Jesus Christ to his followers was that they should love their neighbor as themselves. Jesus did not mean generalized sentimentality or goodwill by this love. For this love to be effective, it has to work through political involvement. Genuine Christian love embraces socio-political action. Christians should not be content with social service. Some cases of need cannot be met at all without political action. As John Stott illustrates, the harsh treatment of slaves could be ameliorated, but not slavery itself; it had to be abolished.

> It is always good to feed the hungry; it is better if possible to eradicate the causes of hunger. So if we truly love our neighbors and want to serve them, our service may oblige us to take (or solicit) political action on their behalf.[56]

In modern societies, the possibility for the people to live the kind of life God intended them to live is profoundly affected by conditions over which individuals and small groups have no control, and by decisions made by a handful of politicians. Thus there must be a political dimension in Christian obedience to the commandment of Jesus Christ to love our neighbor as ourselves.

One of the essential elements of love is concern for others. If some Christians do not have concern for the situation and predicament of others, their profession of faith and their claim to be loyal to their religious principles are suspect. If real Christian faith is not indifferent to the human conditions, the church must show proof of it in its deeds.

> It must be able to make itself heard at the crisis points in the human panorama, there where vital decisions are made, where good and evil are forged, the happiness and misery of men [and women], where the fortune of the world is being built. It is scarcely necessary to add that all this takes place not in the church or the vestry, but above all in the field of politics.[57]

To refuse to be involved in public affairs, therefore, can be a breach of the Great Commandment to love one's neighbor. Christians who really want to obey God must "pursue political activity with a desire to promote justice coupled with a genuine love of neighbor and humility before God."[58]

Dangers in the Political Involvement

We are all weak human beings who have the tendency to go to extremes. When one affirms the necessity of Christian political involvement, some Christians rashly think that politics is "everything" or "the most important thing" in Christian life, and they try to make it the center of life. As Mouw has indicated, there are two common distortions concerning Christian political activity. One is that of the so-called "conservative" Christians, who pay little or no attention to such activity, either by condemning politics as "unchristian" and "unholy," or by completely ignoring the need for political involvement. The other is the attitude found mostly in "liberals," who overemphasize the importance of political activity "to the detriment of other aspects of Christian life and witness."[59] The latter is as bad as the former. As Marshall puts it, "The political order is only one sphere of Christian responsibility before God."[60] Or in Mott's phrase, political activity is "only one in a spectrum of means to justice." Christians must be

> rightly critical of such heavy reliance upon political and economic means to deal with social evil that political action becomes the principal thrust of the church in society. While seeking external controls to resolve social problems, we may come to neglect other aspects of Christian mission.[61]

We should be very cautious not to make the mistake of emphasizing social ethics at the sacrifice of personal ethics. Christian social concern should always be accompanied by an effort for evangelism and nurturing. In no case should Christianity be equated with social humanism, nor should the church be equated with a social action agency, nor should a Christian be a mere humanist.

There is another danger that pertains to individual Christians who seek to hold public office, that is, pursuing power out of one's own selfish ambition. Satisfying one's own desire for power can be the motive for a Christian to run for a public office. Such a Christian would be very likely to confirm the popular understanding that politics is dirty and dishonest and is a conduct of public affairs by which to gain private or partisan advantages. Such Christian politicians would be concerned only about grasping and maintaining power instead of using it to serve and love others.

Just like many other precious things, political power can be a stumbling block for Christian politicians, because to be an influential politician means "being deferred to and being surrounded by a hundred little reminders everyday that you are someone, that you are important." Monsma, who has had considerable experience as a professional politician, describes this factor:

> It means a staff that serves you at your command; it means lobbyists who will entertain and flatter you; it means people who are delighted to get an appointment with you; it means people standing up and applauding when you

> are introduced — or when you simply walk into a room; it means having your name in the headlines and appearing on television and radio; it means being recognized as a person of standing...all this and more.[62]

If a Christian is engaged in politics out of such selfish motives, he or she will unmistakably bring disgrace to the name of Christ and the Church. Christian politicians who begin their careers with a pure objective to glorify God and serve others through politics also should beware of conforming to "politics as usual." The temptations that accompany power are so great that without vigilant self-examination in the light of the Word of God, a Christian politician would merely be consolidating the statement of Norman Mailer when he was considering his new role of candidate for mayor of New York City: "It's very dangerous for your soul to be a politician, because if you get power it can lead you to perdition faster than almost any other form of human activity."[63]

The dangers which accompany the exercise of power, however, are not confined to political power, because the phenomenon of power does not exist exclusively in politics. Power can take various forms: ecclesiastical power, material power, academic power, etc. Therefore, the dangers accompanying political power are universal; they are found wherever the phenomenon of power exists. Any kind of power may be abused. The fact that politics involves dangers accompanied by power cannot be an excuse for Christians to avoid assuming political responsibilities.

The Reformed perspective can help us to keep both the opportunities and the dangers of political power in mind. The Korean Calvinist community has, in this perspective, an important gift to offer to the Korean nation, in which both the opportunities and dangers of political power need very much to be recognized.

1 J. Marcellus Kik, *Church and State: The Story of Two Kingdoms* (Thomas Nelson & Sons: New York, 1963), 115-116.

2 As an exemplary article to support this broader interpretation, see, Leonard W. Levy, "The Original Meaning of the Establishment Clause of the First Amendment," in James E. Wood, Jr. ed. *Religion and State* (Baylor University Press, Waco, Texas, 1985), 43-83.

3 J. M. O'Neill, *Religion and Education Under the Constitution* (New York: Harper and Row, 1949), p. 56. Chester James Antieau, Arthur L. Downey, and Edward C. Roberts, *Freedom and Federal Establishment: Formation and Early History of the First Amendment Religion Clauses* (Milwaukee: Bruce Publishing Company, 1964), is the most completely documented presentation of this point of view, which can also be found in Robert L. Cord, *Separation of Church and State: Historical Fact and Current Fiction* (New York: Lambeth Press, 1984).

4 I draw much of the following discussion on Kik, *Church and State,* 107-116.

5 *Institutes*, IV, xx, 2, 3.

6 Cyril Garbett, *Church and State in England* (London: Hodder and Stoughton, 1950), 13-19.

7 Kik, *Church and State*, 110.

8 Levy, "The Original Meaning," 77, 72-3.

9 *Institutes*, IV, xx, 3.

10 Leo F. Solt, *Church and State in Early Modern England, 1509 - 1640* (Oxford University Press, 1990), 3-4.

11 Thomas G. Sanders, *Protestant Concepts of Church and State* (New York: Holt, Rinehart and Winston, Inc., 1964), 245.

12 Robert Baird, *Religion in America* (New York: Harper & Row, 1856), 178.

13 Louis Weeks, "Faith and Political Action in American Presbyterianism," in Ronald H. Stone, ed. *Reformed Faith and Politics* (Washington D. C.: The University Press of America, 1983), 115.

14 Sanders describes this position of American Calvinists as "transformationism." According to him, the advocates of this position are characterized by "moderation and pragmatism" in their understanding of the Constitutional concept of "separation of Church and State." On

the contrary, absolute separationism is the position of the Baptists who maintains that there should be a "wall" between Church and State. Many Korean Presbyterians' understanding of the proper relation of Church and State seems to be much closer to that of the Baptists rather than to Calvinists.

15 Francis A. Schaeffer, *A Christian Manifesto* (Westchester, Illinois: Crossing Books, 1982), 90.

16 Marshall, *Thy Kingdom Come*, 48-50.

17 David C. Steinmetz, "Calvin and Melanchthon on Romans 13:1-7," *Ex Auditu* (Princeton Theological Seminary, 1986), 80.

18 Schaeffer, 91.

19 Mouw, *Biblical Drama*, 108-9.

20 James D. G. Dunn, "Romans 13:1-7 — A Charter for Political Quietism?," in *Ex Auditu*, 1986, 65.

21 Mott, 150.

22 William Bridge, *The Works of Rev. William Bridge* (Pennsylvania: Soli Deo Gloria, 1989), vol. 5, "The Wounded Conscience Cured, The Weak One Strengthened, and the Doubting Satisfied," 219-220.

23 Marshall, 50.

24 For the further information, see, Schaeffer, *A Christian Manifesto*, 93-99.

25 *Ibid.*, 93.

26 The following is the outline of Schaefferr, *Manifesto*, 99-104.

27 *Ibid.*, 106-7.

28 *Ibid.*, 130.

29 *The Encyclopedia Americana* (Grolier Incorporated, 1988), vol. 8, 591.

30 *Ibid.*, 129.

31 Mark A. Noll, *Christians in the American Revolution* (Christian University Press, 1977), 51.

32 Leonard J. Kramer, "Muskets in the Pulpit, 1776-1783: Part I," *Journal of the Presbyterian Society*, XXXI (September, 1953), 176.

33 Schaeffer, *Manifesto*, 128-9.

34 Christopher Hill, *Intellectual Origins of the English Revolution* (Oxford University Press, 1965), 6.

35 Peter Lewis, "Puritan England," in *The Christian and the State In Revolutionary Times*, 63.
36 Thomas Case, *Two Sermons Lately Preached at Westminster, before Sundry of the Honourable House of Commons* (London, 1641), II, 18.
37 *Ibid.*, 21-22.
38 Mott, 194.
39 Noll, *Christians in the American Revolution*, 30.
40 John Milton, *The Works of John Milton*, vol. 5, *The Tenure of Kings and Magistrates* (New York: Columbia University Press, 1933), 10.
41 *Ibid.*, 14.
42 Christopher Goodman, *How Superior Powers Ought to Be Obeyed* (Geneva, 1558), 139-140.
43 For the more detailed explanation of these conditions, see Mott, 187-190.
44 Schaeffer, *Manifesto*, 124.
45 Fowler, 193.
46 *Ibid.*, 170.
47 Coleman, 193.
48 Coleman, 199-200.
49 Garbett, 296.
50 Marshall, 147.
51 Bong Ho Son, "An Introduction," *Church and State* (Seoul: Institute for the Promotion of Christian Culture, 1988), 16-18.
52 Bong Ho Son's answer to a question in *Modern Church and State* (Seoul: Emmao Publishing Co., 1988), 140.
53 Bong Ho Son, "An Introduction," 18-19.
54 Bong Ho Son, "Church and State from the Perspective of Modern Situation," in *Modern Church and State*, 116-117.
55 Monsma, 60.
56 Stott, 32.
57 B. J. de Clerq, *Religion, ideologie, et politique* (Casterman, Tournai, 1968), 54, quoted by Davies, 29-30.
58 Mouw, *Biblical Drama*, 110.
59 Mouw, *Political Evangelism*, 18.
60 Marshall, 58.

[61] Mott, 197.
[62] Monsma, 23.
[63] Coleman, 185.

Bibliography

Allen, J. W. *A History of Political Thought in the Sixteenth Century*. London: Methuen and Co., 1928.

Aquinas, Thomas. *Summa Theologiae*.

___*On Kingship, to the King of Cyprus*. translated and revised by Gerald B. Phelan and I. Th. Eschmann. Toronto, Pontifical Institutes of Medieval Studies, 1949.

Baird Robert. *Religion in America*. New York: Harper & Row, 1856.

Balke, Willem. *Calvin and the Anabaptist Radicals*, trans. William Heynen. Grand Rapids, Michigan, 1981.

Baron, Hans. "Calvinist Republicanism and Its Historical Roots," *Church History*, 8 (1939).

Berkhof, Hendrikus. *The Doctrine of the Holy Spirit*. Richmond, Virginia: Knox, 1964.

Beza, Theodore. *Concerning the Rights of Rulers over Their Subjects and the Duty of Subjects towards Their Rulers*. ed A H. Murray, tran. Henry Louis Gonin. Cape Town:H.A.U.M., 1956.

___*The Right of Magistrates over Their Subjects* in Julian H. Franklin. *Constitutionalism and Resistance in the Sixteenth Century*. New York, 1969.

Bierce Ambrose. *The Devil's Dictionary*. Mount Vernon, New York: Peter Pauper Press, 1958.

Blair, W. N. *Gold in Korea*. Presbyterian Church in the U. S. A., 1957.

Bonhoeffer, Dietrich. *Ethics*. London: SCM Press, 1955.

Bonnet, Julet, ed. *Letters of John Calvin*. 4 vols. New York, 1972.

Bousma, William. *John Calvin: A Sixteenth Century Portrait*. Oxford University Press, 1988.

Bridge, William. *The Works of Rev. William Bridge,* Vol. 5. Pennsylvania: Soli Deo Gloria, 1989.

Brown, P. Hume. *John Knox*, 2 vols. London: Adam and Charles Black, 1895.

___*John Knox and His Times*. Edinburgh and London: Oliphant, Anderson and Ferrier, 1905.

Burns, J. H. "John Knox and Revolution." *History Today* 8 (Augst, 1958), 565-73.

Busch, Eberhard, "Church and Politics in Reformed Tradition," in James E. Bradley and Richard A. Muller, eds. *Church, Word, and Spirit*. Grand Rapids, Michigan, 1987.

Calvin, John. *Institutes of the Christian Religion*. trans. Ford L. Battles and ed. John McNeill. 2 vols. *The Library of Christian Classics*, vols. XX and XXI. Philadelphia:Westminster Press, 1960

___*Letters of John Calvin*, ed. Jules Bonnet, trans. Marcus R. Gilchrist. New York: Lenox Hill Pub. & Dist. Co.

___*The Commentaries of John Calvin*, Wm. B. Eerdmans Publishing Company.

Case, Thomas. *Two Sermons Lately Preached at Westminster, before Sundry of the Honourable House of Commons*. London, 1641.

Cerillo, Augustus, Jr. and Dempster, Murray W. eds. *Salt and Light: Evangelical Political Thought in Modern America*. Grand Rapids, Michigan: Baker Book House Company, 1989.

Cheneviere, Edouard. *La pensee politique de Calvin*. Geneva, 1937.

Chadwick, W. Owen. "John Knox and Revolution." *Andover Newton Quarterly* 15 (March 1975), 250-66.

Coleman, Richard J. *Issues of Theological Warfare: Evangelicals and Liberals*. Grand Rapids, Michigan: William B. Eerdmans Publishing Co., 1972.

Cord, Robert L. *Separation of Church and State: Historical Fact and Current Fiction*. New York: Lambeth Press, 1984.

Cowan, Henry. *John Knox: The Hero of the Scottish Reformation*. ew York: The Knickerbocker Press, 1905.

Cowan, Ian B. *The Scottish Reformation: Church and Society in ixteenth-century Scotland*. New York: St. Martin's Press, 1982.

Crook, Isaac. *John Knox: The Reformer*. Cincinnati: Jennings and Graham, 1906.

D'Assonville, V. E. *John Knox and the Institutes of Calvin: A Few Points of Contact in Their Theology*. Durban: Drakensberg Press Limited, 1968.

Davies, J. G. *Christians, Politics and Violent Revolution*. London: SCM Press Ltd., 1976.

Dennet, Tyler. "President Roosevelt's Secret Pact with Japan," in *Current History*, vol. 21, No. 1, oct., 1924.

Dickinson, William Croft. *The Scottish Reformation and its Influence upon Scottish Life and Character*. Edinburgh: Saint Andrews Press, 1960.

Doob, Leonard W. *Patriotism and Nationalism*. New Haven, Connecticut: Yale University Press, 1964.

Dunn, James D. G. "Romans 13:1-7 — A Charter for Political Quietism," in *Ex Auditu*. Princeton Theological Seminary, 1986.

Fairbank, John K., Reischauer, Edwin O., and Craig, Allen M. *A History of East Asian Civilization*, vol. II. Boston: Houghton Mifflin Co., 1965.

Figgis, J. N. *Political Thought from Gerson to Grotius: 1414-1625.* New York: Harper and Brothers, 1960.

Fowler, Robert Booth. *A New Engagement: Evangelical Political Thought: 1966-1976*. Grand Rapids, Michigan: William B. Eerdmans Company, 1982.

Fromm, Erich. *The Sane Society*. New York: Rinehart, 1955.

Froom, LeRoy E. *The Prophetic Faith of Our Fathers,* vols. 1, 2. Washington, D. C.: Review and Herald, 1948.

Gamble, Richard C. "The Christian and the Tyrant: Beza and Knox on Political Resistance Theory." *Westminster Theological Journal* 46 (1984), 125-39.

Garbett, *Church and State in England*. London: Hodder and Stoughton, 1950.

Gilck, Calvin C. "Non-Calvinist Influences on the Scottish Reformation," Th.D. diss., Knox College, University of Toronto, 1970.

Glasse, John. *John Knox, a Criticism and an Appreciation.* London: Adam and Chales Black, 1905.

Goodman, Christopher. *How Superior Powers Ought to Be Obeyed*. Geneva, 1558.

Graham, W. Fred. *The Constructive Revolutionary John Calvin*. Michigan State University Press, 1987.

Grajdanzev, Andrew J. *Modern Korea*. New York: John Day Co., 1944.

Gray, John R. "The Political Theory of John Knox." *Church History* 8 (June 1939), 132-147.

Greaves, Richard L. *Theology and Revolution in the Scottish Reformation: Studies in the Thought of John Knox*. Grand Rapids: Christian University Press, 1980.

___"John Knox, the Reformed Tradition, and the Development of Resistance Theory." *The Journal of Modern History* 48 (1976), 1-35.

Griffin, Keith L., "Reluctant Revolutionaries: The Middle Colony Reformed Idea of a Just Resistance," Ph. D. dissertation, Fuller Theological Seminary, 1989.

Hearshaw, F. J. C. *The Social and Political Ideas of Some Great Thinkers of the Renaissance and the Reformation*. London, 1925.

Henderson, G. D. ed. and intro. *The Scots Confession of 1560*. Edinburgh: Saint Andrew press, 1960.

Hill, Christopher. *Intellectual Origins of English Revolution*. Oxford University Press, 1965.

Hoepfl, Harro. *The Christian Polity of John Calvin*. Cambridge University Press, 1982.

Hoffman, Manfred. "Martin Luther: Resistance to Secular Authority," *The Journal of International Theological Center* 12, Fall, 1984/Spring, 1985.

Hulbert, Homer B. *The Passing of Korea*. New York: Doubleday, Page & Company, 1906.

Johnston, O. R. *Nationhood: towards a Christian Perspective*. Oxford: Latimer House, 1980.

Jungen, Christopher. "Calvin and the Origin of Political Resistance Theory in the Calvinist Tradition," Th. M. Thesis, westminster Theological Seminary, 1980.

Kik, J. Marcellus. *Church and State: The Story of Two Kingdoms*. New York: Thomas Nelson & Sons, 1963.

Kingdon, R. M., *Geneva and the Coming of Wars of Religion in France, 1555-1563*. Geneva, 1956.

___"The Political Resistance of the Calvinists in France and the Low Countries," *Church History*, 27 (1958).

___"The First Expression of Theodore Beza's Political Ideas," *Archiv fur Reformationsgeschichte*, 46 (1955). 88-99.

Knox, John. *The Works of John Knox*. 6 vols. Edited by David Laing. Edinburgh: Printed for the Bannatyne Club, 1846-1864.

Koenigsberger, H. G., and George L. Mosse. *Europe in the Sixteenth Century*. New York: Holt, Rinehart and Winston, Inc., 1968.

Korean National Council of Churches. *The Movement for the Democratization in 1970s*, vol. I. Seoul: Committee of Human Rights of KNCC, 1987.

Kyle, Richard, G. *The Mind of John Knox*. Lawrence: Coronado Press, 1984.

___"The Church-State Patterns in the Thought of John Knox." *Journal of Church and State* 30, No. 1 (winter 1988) 71-87.

___"John Knox: The Main Themes of His Thought." *The Princeton Seminary Bulletin* 4, No. 2 (1983), 101-111.

Lang, Andrew. *John Knox and the Reformation*. London: Longmans, Green and Co., 1905.

Langford, Norman F. "Christians and Politics," *Church and Society*, 62 (1972).

Leith, John H. *Introduction to the Reformed Tradition: A Way of Being the Christian Community*. Atlanta, Georgia: John Knox Press, 1981.

Levy, Leonard W. "The Original Meaning of the Establishment Clause of the First Amendment," *Religion and State*. James E. Wood, Jr. ed. Waco, Texas: Baylor University Press, 1985.

Lewis, Peter. "Puritan England," *The Christian and the State in Revolutionary Times*. Huntingdon, Cambs.: The Westminster Conference 1975.

Little, David. *Religion, Order and Law*. The University of Chicago Press, 1984.

___"Reformed Faith and Religious Liberty." *Church and Society*, May/June 1986, 6-28.

Lloyd, H. A., "Calvin and the Duty of Guardians to Resist," in *Journal of Ecclesiastical History*, vol. 32, No. 1, Jan. 1981.

McNeill, John.T. *History and Character of Calvinism*. Oxford University Press, 1954.

___"The Democratic Element in Calvin's Thought," *Church History* 18 (1949).

___"Calvin and Civil Government," in Donald K. McKim. ed. *Readings in Calvin's Theology*, Grand Rapids, Michigan, 1984.

___"John Calvin on Civil Government," in George L. Hunter, ed. *Calvinism and the Political Order*. Philadelphia, 1964.

Luther, Martin. "Secular Authority: To What Extent It Should be Obeyed," *Martin Luther: Selection from His Writings*. John Dillenberger, ed., New York: Doubleday, 1961.

M'Crie, Thomas. *Life of John Knox.* 2 vols. Philadelphia: Presbyterian Board of Publication, 1831.

MacGregor, Geddes. *The Thundering Scot: A Portrait of John Knox.* Philadelphia: The Westminster Press, 1957.

Mackenzie, Agnes Mure. *The Scotland of Queen Mary and the Religious Wars, 1513-1638*. Edinburgh: A. Maclehose and Co., 1936.

MacLeod, George F. *John Knox and Today.* Geneva: The John Knox Association, 1959.

Marshall, Paul. *Thine is the Kingdom: A Biblical Perspective on the Government and Politics Today*. Grand Rapids, Michigan: William B. Eerdmans Publishing Company, 1984.

Masahiko, Kurata. *A History of the Japanese Persecution of Korean Church*. Seoul: The Christian Literature Press, 1991.

Mathieson, William Law. *Politics and Religion: A Study in Scottish History from the Reformation to the Revolution*. 2 vols. Glasgow: James Maclehose and Sons, 1902.

May, Rolly. *The Art of Counseling*. New York: Abingdon, 1939.

McRoberts, David, ed. *Essays on the Scottish Reformation, 1513-1625*. Glasgow: John S. Burns and Sons, 1962.

Miller, Perry. *Errand into the Wilderness*. Cambridge: The Balknap Press of Harvard University Press, 1956.

Milton, John. *The Works of John Milton*, Vol. 5, *The Tenure of Kings and Magistrates*. New York: Columbia University Press, 1933.

Monsma, Stephen V. *Pursuing Justice in a Sinful World*. Grand Rapids, Michigan: William B. Eerdmans Publishing Co., 1984.

Mott, Stephen Charles. *Biblical Ethics and Social Change*. Oxford University Press, 1982.

Mouw, Richard J. *Political Evangelism*. Grand Rapids, Michigan: William B. Eerdmans Publishing Company, 1973.

___*Politics and the Biblical Drama*. Grand Rapids, Michigan: William B. Eerdmans Publishing Company, 1976.

___*God Who Commands*. Notre Dame University Press, 1990.

Mueller, William A., *Church and State in Luther and Calvin*. Nashville, Tenessee: Broadman Press, 1954.

Muhn, Jungchang. *A Korean History of Thirty Six Years under the Militaristic Japan*. Seoul: Paikmuhndang, 1966.

Muir, Edwin. *John Knox: Portrait of a Calvinist*. Edinburgh: J. and J.Gray, 1929.

Niebuhr, H. Richard. *The Kingdom of God in America*. New York: Harper, 1937.

Noll, Mark A. *Christians in the American Revolution.* Washington D. C. : Christian University Press, 1977.

O'Neill, J. M. *Religion and Education Under the Constitution*. New York: Harper and Row, 1949.

Paik, L. George. *The History of Protestant Missions in Korea: 1832-1910*. Seoul: Yonsei University Press, 1980.

Percy, Lord Eustace. *John Knox*. Richmond: John Knox Press, 1966.

Rees, Paul. "Prayer and Social Concern," in *The Chicago Declaration*. ed. Ronald J. Sider, Carol Stream, Illinois: Creation House, 1974.

Reid, W. Stanford. *Trumpeter of God: A Biography of John Knox.* New York: Charles Scribner's Son, 1974.

___"John Knox's Theology of Political Government." *The Sixteenth Century Journal* 19, No. 4 (1988), 529-540.

Ridley, John. *John Knox*. Oxford University Press, 1968.

Ridley, Jasper. *John Knox*. New York: Oxford University Press, 1968.

Roberts, Edward C. *Freedom and Federal Establishment: Formation and the Early History of the First Amendment Religion Clauses*. Milwaukee: Bruce Publishing Company, 1964.

Rottenberg, Isaac C., "The Shape of the Church's Social-Economic Witness," in *Reformed Journal* 27 (May, 1977).

Rupp, E. G. "The Europe of John Knox," in *John Knox: A Quartercentenary Reappraisal*. ed. Duncan Shaw. Edinburgh: The Saint Andrews Press, 1975.

Russell, E. "John Knox as Statesman." *The Princeton Theological Review* 6, No. 1 (Jan. 1908), 1-28.

Sanders, Thomas G. *Protestant Concept of Church and State*. New York: Holt, Rinehart and Winston Inc.,

Schaeffer, Fransis A. *A Christian Manifesto*. Westchester, Illinois: Crossing Books, 1982.

Schelven, A. A. van. "Beza's De Iure Magistratuum in Subditos." *Archiv fur Reformatyionsgeschichte* 45 (1954), 62-83.

Shaw, Duncan. "John Knox and Mary, Queen of Scots," in *John Knox: A Quartercentenary Reappraisal*. Edinburgh: The Saint Andrew Press, 1975

___*Reformation and Revolution*. Edinburgh: Saint Andrew Press, 1967.

Skinner, Quentin. *The Foundations of Modern Political Thought*. Cambridge University Press.,1978

Smedes, Lewis B. "What do We Differ," in *Reformed Journal* 16 (May-June, 1966).

___"The Evangelical and the Social Question," in *Reformed Journal* 16 (February, 1966).

Smith, A. D. *Theories of Nationalism*. Duckworth, 1971.

Smith, Timothy L. *Revivalism and Social Reform in Mid-Nineteenth Century America*. New York: Abingdon, 1957.

Solt, Leo F. *Church and State in Early Modern England: 1509-1640*. Oxford University Press, 1990.

Solzhenitsyn, Alexander. *One Word of Truth*. New York: Farrar, Straus and Giroux, 1971.

Stalker, James. *John Knox: His Ideas and Ideals*. London: Hodder and Stoughton, 1904.

Steinmetz, David C. "Calvin and Melanchthon on Romans 13:1-7," in *Ex Aditu*. Princeton Theological Seminary, 1986.

Stott, John R. W. *Involvement: Being A Responsible Christian in a Non-Christian Society*. Old Teppan, New Jersey: Fleming H. Revell Company, 1984.

Sutherland, N. "Calvinism and the Conspiracy of Amboise," *History*, 47 (1962).

Swallen, W. L. "God's Work of Grace at Pyeng Yang Classes," in *Korea Mission Field*, vol. 3, No. 5.

Thomson, Cargill. "Luther and the Right of Resistance to the Emperor," *Church, Society, and Politics*. 1975.

VanderMolen, Ronald. "Political Calvinism," *Journal of Church and State*, 11 (1969).

Vesey, W. J. "The Sources of the Idea of Active Resistance in the Political Theory of John Knox." Ph. D. diss., Boston University, 1961.

Vos, Clarence J. "Human Authority: A Biblical Study with a comparison of Calvin's view," in David E. Holwerda, ed. *Exploring the Heritage of John Calvin*. Grand Rapids, Michigan, 1976.

Walzer, Michael. *The Revolution of the Saints: A Study in the Origins of Radical Politics*. Harvard University Press, 1965.

Watt, Hugh. *John Knox in Controversy*. New York: Philosophical Library, 1950.

Weeks, Louis. "Faith and Political Action in American Presbyterianism," *Reformed Faith and Politics*. Ronald H. Stone, ed. Washington D. C.: The University Press of America, 1983.

Williams, George H. *The Radical Reformation*. Philadelphia: The Westminster Press, 1962.

Wolin, Sheldon. S., *Politics and Vision*. Boston, 1960.

Wormald, Jenny. *Court, Kirk, and Community: Scotland, 1470 -1625*. Toronto: University of Toronto Press, 1981.

Yoder, Howard. *The Politics of Jesus*. Grand Rapids, Michigan: William B. Eerdmans Publishing Company, 1972.

Zagorin, Perez. *Rebels and Rulers 1500-1600*, vol. 1. New York: Cambridge University Press, 1982.

Zuck, Lowell H., ed. *Christianity and Revolution: Radical Christian Testimonies, 150-1650*. Temple University Press, Philadelphia, 1975.

ASIAN THOUGHT AND CULTURE

This series is designed to cover three inter-related projects:

- *Asian Classics Translation*, including those modern Asian works that have been generally accepted as "classics"
- *Asian and Comparative Philosophy and Religion*, including excellent and publishable Ph.D. dissertations, scholarly monographs, or collected essays
- *Asian Thought and Culture in a Broader Perspective*, covering exciting and publishable works in Asian culture, history, political and social thought, education, literature, music, fine arts, performing arts, martial arts, medicine, etc.

For additional information about this series or for the submission of manuscripts, please contact:

Peter Lang Publishing, Inc.
Acquisitions Department
275 Seventh Avenue, 28th floor
New York, New York 10001